CRYBABY!

CRYBABY!

Janice Williamson

*For Chris.
wishing you wonderful
words of your own.
Janice.
October 1998.*

NeWest Press

Edmonton

CANADIAN CATALOGUING IN PUBLICATION DATA

Williamson, Janice.
  Crybaby!

  ISBN 1-896300-36-7

  I. Title.
PS8595.I5653C79   1998   C818'.5407   C98-910683-7
PR9199.3.W4925C79   1998

Editor for the press: Douglas Barbour
Cover and text design: Val Speidel Design
Cover photograph from the collection of the Author

NeWest Press gratefully acknowledges the support of the Department of Canadian Heritage, Canada Council for the Arts for our publishing program and The Alberta Foundation for the Arts (a beneficiary of the Lottery Fund of the Government of Alberta) for its publishing program.

THE CANADA COUNCIL | LE CONSEIL DES ARTS
FOR THE ARTS | DU CANADA
SINCE 1957 | DEPUIS 1957

Printed and bound in Canada

NeWest Publishers Limited
Suite 201, 8540-109 Street
Edmonton, Alberta T6G 1E6

Contents

The only book that is worth writing is the one we don't have the courage or strength to write. I don't want to write the true book; it's the one I want to write: to tear it from myself.

HÉLÈNE CIXOUS

Shadow seemed to lie across the page. It was a straight dark bar, a shadow shaped something like the letter "I." One began dodging this way and that to catch a glimpse of the landscape behind it. . . . One began to be tired of "I." Not but what this "I" was a most respectable "I"; honest and logical; as hard as a nut, and polished for centuries by good teaching and good feeding. I respect and admire that "I" from the bottom of my heart. But—here I turned a page or two, looking for something or other—the worst of it is that in the shadow of the letter "I" all is shapeless as mist.

VIRGINIA WOOLF

Writing isn't just telling stories. It's exactly the opposite. It's telling everything at once. It's the telling of a story and the absence of the story. It's telling a story through its absence…. And so this book, which I'd have liked to resemble a motorway going in all directions at once, will merely be a book that tries to go everywhere but goes to just one place at a time; which turns back and sets out again the same as everyone else, the same as every other book. The only alternative is to say nothing. But that can't be written down.

MARGUERITE DURAS

Crybaby!

Like this exclamation mark of the violence done to you.

BPNICHOL

cry   *L. quiritare,* to raise a plaintive cry, to wail, scream, shriek out, cry aloud, bewail, lament. orig (according to Varro) to implore the aid of the Quirites or Roman citizens.

crybaby   (1851) one who cries or complains easily or often. A derisive appellation for one who cries childishly. *1882 Advance 18 May 317: Tom called him crybaby because his eyes were always filled with tears.* 1889 Sat. Rev. 21 Feb 230/1, "I declare . . . that they are cry-baby chaps."

To cry is to address a listener. The crybaby's song goes not unheard but unheeded; not only the story of woe but the desire to be heard warrants condemnation. Why is it that an appeal for justice or a simple lend-me-your-ear/shoulder to cry on, provokes insult and dismissal? The wronged woman and the abused child speak out and are repudiated. The voice of the crybaby sounds falsetto through history. A "cry-baby chap," feminized by complaint and sorrow, masquerades in his "womanly" self. The perception of feminine or childish excess remakes her as the pitiful abject object. The crybaby suffers out loud and in so doing she is translated from "troubled" to being "in trouble."

(Trust the cry and the crybaby!)

The language of pain is difficult to transmit; it is the glorious nature of civilization to reject suffering. And yet, the suffering of some is more deserving of recognition.

At a reading of *crybaby*, the few people who attend leave the room in silence. Devastated by what I perceive as indifference or disdain, a friend consoles me with Simone Weil's question: *What is the reason that as soon as one human being shows he needs another (no matter whether his need be slight or great) the latter draws back from him?* And her answer?

Gravity.

If I'm going to continue writing, I will need to gain altitude.

EVEN CRYBABIES REMEMBER

To recollect is *to gather again*. When I look up the word *collect* in my dictionary, I find:

> com- + legere   *to gather, select, read more at* LEGEND;
> *akin to Gk* legein *to gather, say* logos *speech, word, reason.*

Stories are gathered from memory and told in images and words that leave tracks somewhere between imagination and history.

This book lives on the borderlands of the prairies, on the outskirts of urban central Canada and in a northern city where the central interpretive devices of our culture may not quite work. Childhood is at the centre—a fifties childhood, my personal past, disrupted by the childhood I recollect as an adult. Looking back, I read the black and white ghosts of family photographs—to find the shadowy traces of my mother in the shadowy face that looks at the photographer through the car window and in her high heel pump abandoned beside my tricycle. I see the father I remember, a man who found he could not live long.

This book is also about a collective history longer than my own—one that begins with Freud's Dora. And about the present—my writing—and how I come to tell my story to you.

Snapshots

The camera saves a set of appearances from the otherwise inevitable supercession of further appearances. It holds them unchanging. And before the invention of the camera nothing could do this, except, in the mind's eye, the faculty of memory.

JOHN BERGER

Somewhere someone has taken my identity and replaced it with a photograph.

THERESA HAK KYUNG CHA

The family photograph is a ritual of the domestic cult in which the family is both subject and object.... If we bear in mind the fact that there is a very close correlation between the presence of children in the household and possession of a camera, and that the camera is often the common property of the family group, it becomes clear that photographic practice only exists and subsists for most of the time by virtue of its family function or rather by the function conferred upon it by the family group, namely that of solemnizing and immortalizing the high points of family life, in short, of reinforcing the integration of the family group by reasserting the sense that it has both of itself and of its unity.

PIERRE BOURDIEU

X 9620

This waiting
for the buddie
for some camera
to the camera

Mom 29/5/51

OUT OF THE CAMERA ERA

IN A HALF DREAM STATE,
THE FIRST TELLING

comes out of my skin like a smell, out of this bed like a shiver, through my spine like a tremor or shake.

March 29, 1989: I awaken at 2:30 A.M., glance at the clock to get my bearings, hear the whine of truck tires itching for traction, and the creak, crash of wood. Silence for a moment, burst open by the grind of truck shifting gears and position, more tire whine and wood wail. I lie motionless, think about calling the police. My mind panic freezes my body unmoved, unmoving. The sense of urgency defined by fear not action. I talk myself out of my senses, imagine my hearing no more than paranoia.

The morning brings no memory of these anxious echoes. Coffee in hand, I get started most days remembering my dreams. This day is no different. I sit at my desk to begin writing a book of "tell tale signs." Dreams play along the moment of recollection too close for comfort. Retracing the liminal, I resurrect the crash of my backyard fence. Ever analytical, I muse about the strangeness of my paranoia: why imagine vandalism at home the night after teaching lesbian love poems in my upper-level undergraduate class? As though to reassure myself there is no connection between my dream and my work life, I glance above the computer monitor. My look slips out the sliding glass doors past the rose garden in winter to gasp at the ripped down mass of lumber and jagged posts. These remnants of my fence are not a nightmare, but a morning awakened to my body's power to forget nocturnal violations. My mental/physical paralysis/erasure leads me to query what it means to remember and how it is we become this forgetting.

SCRAPS OF PROSE ALL I CAN MANAGE.

Moving words from one page to the next reduces the story to snapshots.

A blank spot in the middle.

MONTHS LATER, THE SECOND TELLING
COMES OUT OF MY HEAD

like a slide show. Between the right ear lobe and temple, a slit opens up. No blizzard obscures the straight-ahead traffic of Edmonton Trail. Blinded by the image of a photographic slide framed by white cardboard, I pull over to the side of the highway. As intense as a waking dream, nothing to do but look through the lens of my mind, now projector. Only his back is visible. A man stands in front of a bassinet or changing table, the whiteness of the plastic quilted to embroidered shadow. He is touching the baby somewhere: her genitals? Is this memory no more than a crossover from that elsewhere? Closing my eyes, I shake my head, but the image persists.

Wait.

Like a photograph, this moment freezes into instant appearances. *Habit now protects us against the shock involved in such preservation.*

This image of childhood violation shifts ground in my body from vague anxious fears to various corridors of pain. My vagina aches without reason and all day long I smell shit as though a dog were in every corner, or under the stairs. Smell it everywhere under my skin, this mixture of mental debris and lived surfaces.

I can't remember.

(Does she lie?)

Tiny feet enraged kick off a baby girl's white quilt. Dreaming lions and tigers escape through cracks in the wood floor. The white lace of the blanket catches in the futile directions of a top-hatted animal tamer who dies like all the others. *Momma. Daddy.*

In the waking dream, a dark-haired faceless man is outlined in the window, his hands strangely turned and moving. Infant legs flail out against the mystery.

IN THE CEDAR V OF THE MOUNTAINS, I BEGIN TO NARRATE A STORY

that follows the strict editorial guidelines of Harlequin Industries. Floating through the window, I hope to recognize "the facts" that surface after thirty-seven years.

Maybe it happened in the hotel your grandfather owned. We lived there when you were three, my mother hypothesized on the telephone.

I travel to Nelson in the Kootenays to find out what I can in this place.

But which hotel? I muse fitfully. *Was it the Hume, now renamed The Heritage Hotel, with its long encrusted history of stained glass and buried balustrades? Or was my sense of connection to these 10-foot fireplaces no more than an inflation of my modest class origins? Do I remember my childhood self in The Old Nelson, formerly The New Grand, whose painted-over deco signs had looked across the harbour before three-storey buildings interrupted the view? Or was my child self at play behind the reception desk now hidden behind sliding doors in The Royal Hotel? Drunks in the Royal's saloon mimic the sombre, bearded men photographed on the wall; slumped across tables, their half-closed eyes mime wood-sidewalk stories of too long ago.*

Later on the phone, my mother confirms that we all lived in The Royal.

But The Royal's a dive.

Yes it always was, but the miners were nice and looked after you.

I dive deep down into this "looked after." Thick fists pound at the door as memory crashes into the middle of the hotel room. Drunk, the dark-haired miner stumbles forward to snatch me from my grandmother's arms.

Nanna explains, *The prospectors liked you and always gave you gold nuggets.*

My mother elaborates, *There was one miner especially who missed his family. He really loved you and even babysat. We wouldn't leave you with the other men. They wouldn't have known what to do with you.*

Always watch your backgrounds. They can make or break your pictures.

JULY 9, 1991

This morning I write a story that will help me find my way into my proposed book, a cultural study of West Edmonton Mall. Hardly a new project since I've been thrashing around in it for several years now ever since my move west, giving papers, writing articles, scribbling fictional bits and making videos and photographs.

Here in the mountains, the project feels remote from me. I am supposed to be studying women, shopping, and the mall as a palace of consumption. But why do I care? As a teenager, I hated growing up on the margins of Toronto where the rural would soon be hemmed in by asphalt parking lots. Glorious trees disappeared like the four-room schoolhouse I attended outside the village of Pickering. Why do I care? I hate shopping centres. Why the obsession with The Mall? So it's large and looming, one of the biggest in the world, and filled with a life-size plastic replica of the *Santa Maria*, deadly roller coasters, statues of prostitutes and wave pools. It's a suburban carnival of the new world, but what's the personal attraction?

I close my eyes and start to move my fingers across the keyboard as though automatic writing might provide a clue. *Jelly babies*, they tap out. *Daddy's girl*, they continue, and then nothing. Beginning again, I take the two gifts and turn them into a story only half my own. I write without stopping:

> *Father provided his own kind of shopping pleasures. An absent father like many of his generation, he sent me running from him in tears—"making strange," mother later explained. But even in estrangement there were exceptional moments of pleasure. In the evening or on a Saturday, he would take me on his shoulders and parade through the local Hudson's Bay Store he managed. I*

would wear a smart new dress my mother had made. As we promenaded by the candy counters, women would coo about my good-little-girl looks, pressing gum balls and jelly babies into my sticky palms. My bangs were cut short and precise and in my lofty position under hot store lights, warmed by embarrassed pride, I could feel them wet against my forehead. This was my memory of father/daughter pleasure, an economy of gifts outside everyday exchange. On these shopping expeditions I could play the princess of gracious receiving.

When pressed into shape, certain words float to the surface. I lift up some of the words as though playing with a magic screen where language floats its own secrets.

Father provided his own kind of pleasures … he sent me

running from him in tears … exceptional moments of

pleasure … take me … his shoulders … parade through …

candy … coo … good-little-girl … pressing … balls …

jelly … into my sticky palms … hot … warmed …

embarrassed … wet against my forehead … this memory of

father/daughter pleasure … an everyday exchange …

I could play the princess of gracious receiving …

SHE'S
WAIT-
ING
FOR
THE
BIRDIE
TO
COME

Story-telling sequence pictures are highly effective when **the star is a child.** This **off-to-bed series is a good example of the technique** and its simplicity. The four pictures—clothes being placed in laundry hamper, **hide-and-seek, donning of pajamas, and crib scene** may have little in the way of **dramatic plot** but they are full of human interest. Such a series of sequence shots, interesting when taken, becomes **priceless as time passes.**

Figure 1 Nowadays, the aim of a family photo is to show members as they really are, natural and unposed. In such pictures the camera is ignored as the subjects relax and attempt to be themselves.

WHO IS BEHIND THE CAMERA?
A LOVING FATHER?

These photographs are not about finding "the truth" of my childhood. They are a childhood. A possible account. Whether my father molested me will not be established. My memory has proven resilient in its ability to find an equilibrium somewhere between vision and articulation, a zone of possible plots, likely scenarios, blurred images. Gaps and fissures, arguments and echoes make up what I know about this child who stands before me. Her fingers curve up like wings.

> Many things are right about this picture.
>
> Notable is the angle from which it is shot.
>
> A low angle makes viewer participant and
>
> provides plain background.

Figure 2 Migrating east from the prairies, I pose with certainty about my status as only child. In the photograph, I squint into the sun. My right hand extends out to the camera. His mustached smile widens for the camera's (my mother's) eye. On the tricycle or perched in the car door, poised and confident, I am Daddy's girl. Mother hovers at the edge of the frame. Peering through the car window, does she catch a glimpse of "something funny"?

THE PHOTOGRAPHS BURN INTO MEMORY.

A familial branding. Pictures of the happiest of times when his words of paternal love inscribe themselves on the other side of black and white images. The three-year-old girl delighted in his attentions looks out from the 1953 Dodge with the premature pride of ownership. See the careening swing, the tricycle curving past my mother's high-heeled shoe in the hotel's courtyard.

In these photographs, I am the well-groomed child, nattily dressed in 1950s middle-class comfort. Mother and I followed father from the prairies to seek fortune in the prosperous east where he manages the Hudson Bay department store in Ajax, Ontario, a model post-war industrial small town. A big enough fish, father will eventually establish himself as a sometimes too-zealous and unethical entrepreneur who, in 1973, will lose his business to an American takeover. An All-Canadian story of branch-plant downsizing economics. But for the moment, in 1953, his charm and aggressive ambition are about to propel him into his dreams.

My father has a powerful voice. Is the voice hidden in his throat or thrown from somewhere else, a ventriloquist's fiction?

What if we answer, *Yes!*

Will his lips tremble?

When do his hands begin to shake?

THE FAMILY ALBUM REMEMBERS

In place of **bigness**, the new album emphasizes compactness. Instead of one or two big, bulky books, the modern picture collector maintains a number of **smaller** volumes, uniform in size and appearance but with relatively few pages. Each book is devoted to a specific subject—such as any year's vacation, a trip, the building of the house, military or civilian defence duties, "Junior," "The Kids," the garden, family hobbies—and so on and on.

Figure 3 *Children: Being like young animals, children are popular as photographic subjects—especially, and understandably enough, among parents who like to keep their offsprings' early looks recorded.*

IN ITS PRESENTATION OF IDENTITY

*(**that** person, **that** place) standing before us, the photo is incontrovertible, while the poem, less presence than presentiment, runs a sort of controversy between what can be identified and what remains nameless, what has been said and what is yet unsayable.*

---

the captioned photograph

is a poem

Figure 4 This photograph is not documentary

This photograph is a visual signal of the unsayable. The story of incest may be hidden from him. The handwriting is familiar but these family photographs are not incontrovertible. The certainty of identity marked by visual likeness is unsettled and made ambiguous by his words.

MOTHER TAKES THE PHOTOGRAPH

Your can show yourself in a reckless role by the judicious use of paste and scissors, plus a few pictures.... This composite photo technique has been used over the years for many purposes, some amusing, some fraudulent, but most of them quite legitimate. It was once the hallmark of a particularly lurid brand of journalism. If the newspaper couldn't get legitimate photographs it manufactured them out of stock photos, artwork, paste pot, and scissors. Photographs of this sort have turned up repeatedly in courts of law but the composite has many legitimate uses. It is often used in advertising. With it an automobile manufacturer can show a giant holding one of his cars in his hand, presumably considering its fine points. Or, conversely, with this technique a swarm of Lilliputian housewives can be depicted as they inspect a new range or refrigerator, admiring various and sundry features.

Figure 5 Father wears his new suit to pose for the camera. Mother has made my dress, white cotton and simple Peter-Pan collar. The little white sweater knit by my great aunt looks like a lamb. In my white dress, I am awkwardly posed; my body shifts towards the edge of the frame. Father is the focal point. Anticipating affirmation, he writes on the back of the photograph: *My but don't I look healthy.*

... Daddy's girl.

. . . OR MOMMY'S GIRL?

The trick is to align both figures so that the distant one appears to be a doll manipulated by the person in the foreground. A common version of this shows the background figure being held doll-like, in the palm of the hand of the person close to the camera, but this basic idea **can be given many variations**.

Figure 6 Like a lamb, I stare out at my mother who holds the camera. My hand rests on father's knee. Mother shifts to focus the lens on father who takes up his central place. The girl, me, edges towards the frame. This is as it should be. Snap. Shot. Children should be almost seen. His torso leans towards her, hand covering his genitals. This fatherly figure is at the centre of the photograph: see the carefully bobbed hair and bangs. A door, the hotel door, swings closed behind his right shoulder.

A PRECISE PETER-PAN COLLAR ANCHORS
HER PALE RUMPLED CARDIGAN.

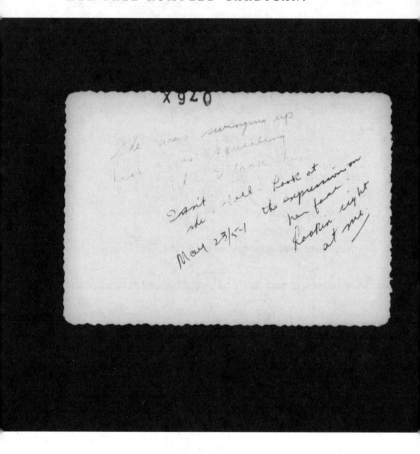

Figure 7 He writes on the back of the photograph taken three weeks after my third birthday. The scrawled script appears granular as though written in sand. The orthography is familiar, but the photograph takes on ominous meanings. In this image, I am invisible to myself, though the edges of the child distinguish me from what I am not. Her/my being is not mine.

IT DOESN'T TAKE LONG. I CUT MYSELF OUT OF HIS BODY.

Repossess my own. I want to make my boundaries that I longed for, the edges shirred or sharp. First I scan the image into the machine. In revising the photograph, I can make myself disappear. The blank space in the foreground marks the distance from my child body, the space pain makes. I take the little girl first, lasso myself right out of my father's photograph. All my edges are fluffy. My torso, indistinct on the left side, blends into the white-frilled border. When the girl/I disappears, the remainder of the photograph tells a story of retribution. She/I takes part of father with her. The girl's arm, now absent, cuts into her father's leg like a sword.

I take another photograph and line up the edges of father's body with the computer's stylus. A wavy dotted line outlines his silhouette on the screen. I flick a key; he disappears. This is as it should be. The little girl stands near the frame of the photograph. Is she puzzled by the absent centre? Or relieved? This photograph is not documentary evidence, but a sign of the unsayable. *The impact of incest may be hidden from him.*

THE I AM IS GIVEN ITS TIME
IN WHICH TO REFLECT ON THE PAST

> *and to anticipate its future: the exposure time does no
> violence to the time of the I am: on the contrary, one
> has the strange impression that the exposure time is the
> lifetime.*

I look into the photograph as if it were a camera. The girl in
the photograph looks out at me as though remembering then
and now. The photographs speak to me of a life process
rooted in this child's body which extends from the click of
the camera's eye towards these fingers at the keyboard.
Though I recall the pillars, the terrace, the block glass windows of Whitby's Spruce Villa Hotel where we lived in 1954,
looking back into the photograph from this point in time I
see how my family is located on the move today, gone tomorrow, ascending into more permanent house rites. Nomadic
turned suburban. Not quite precise. At sixteen, I will run
away from home, from the proximity of the paternal, the dis-
tinguished entranceway pillars.

THIS WRITING

makes
me
inadequate
to
the
task
of
story
i
rush
on
fearful
of
seduction's
sweet
spin
words
read
themselves
on
the
page
the
strip
of
self-disclosure
looped
circuit
of
looking/being
looked
at

makes
this
i
nomadic

alive anywhere
but behind these eyes

PEEK! HE WRITES ON THE BACK OF
HER PHOTOGRAPH.

He puts words in her mouth. I longed for him in my dreams …

… first she takes off her pants
(black cotton, straight-legged, simple buckle, black leather)
her belt slides along
the girl takes off her pants,
one leg,
then another
her socks come off too

[first she takes off her pants]

the crinkle of plastic or
squeal of rubber
once upon a time
when she was a little girl
her rubber pants made a sound
when rubbed, she squealed

dreaming she takes off her pants,
she imagines his hands,
the crinkle of squeal

[the figure in the sentence "she takes off her pants" does
not escape her]

she makes love
with her mouth
open
anxious,
like a bird

How many times do I dream of this?
Is once upon a time enough?

IT IS BEYOND THE SHOCK OF BEING STRICKEN,

> *but nonetheless within the wound and from within the woundedness that the event, incomprehensible though it may be, becomes accessible.*

One mother's story recounts the horror of confronting her husband: she writes beyond the anticipated endings of complicity or collusion, impotence or rage. Her daughter writes back to her with a bitter intelligence and love.

Too close for comfort, she felt abandoned.

TRAUMA SEVERS MY RIGHT HAND; MY PEN HAS A MIND OF HER OWN.

I travel in order to write. Or stay home in order to write. In order to write, move the computer into a different room, rearrange the files. On the snow-filled afternoon, go for a walk to write. Today drink coffee before and after writing: during does not occur. You don't want to write a word. Feels it is bad to organize yourself this way. The years of finding yourself in this *roomtalking*. As a child, you will not tell. Speaking. Not speaking. Telling. Not. You talk too much. This little girl won't shut up. You talk over the other students, interrupt the teacher. Can't stop in the middle of a sentence since you've already jumped ahead into another. Talks too much—excellent student, but she talks and talks and talks....

WHAT IS MY RESISTANCE TO WRITING?

Aversion:

1. to feign illness or arrange an accidental drowning at sea;
2. to long for a fancy aeronautical tragedy or a grave of red sand;
3. to develop time-zone disorder comprised of prairie disequilibrium (and a little librium).

(Nothing sounds plausible.)

Aversion. Voila. Voyeur. If you please. My desire: to watch television talk shows about children who murder their parents, girls who go wrong and still get their way. Women who do not regret killing abusive husbands.

One woman says: *He beat me for six years. He sexually abused my daughters. We separated. He broke into our home. I was afraid for my daughters. I shot him once in the belly as he came through the window. He died.*

I kissed him on the lips, she cries. *I still love him.*

If you had to do it over again, would you pull the trigger? asks the interviewer.

The murderer interrupts her tears, incredulous: Are you kidding? Of course I would shoot him again.

I AM MADE STRANGE TO MYSELF.

We wrap our babies in love and find them uncradled, undone by another's desire. Swaddled in the bleach of innocence, always already vulnerable, the child succumbs to infection. We treat her with kid gloves, ignore symptoms, until she grow up diseased and wanting. She waits for someone to witness her suffering. Remember how night cries crest at the edge of betrayal, eyes wide with unimaginable terror of gargantuan limbs. Remember invasive flesh under a microscope, an infant's gaze. Borders between bodies open and close to touch, crushed under pressure of hand or chest or groin.

Figure 8 *To testify is to encounter—and make you encounter—strangeness.* I write I did not experience incest and feel abject, ashamed at my lack of courage. I write nothing, and am saddened by the blank page. I write nonsense and am aggrieved by this play of dissimulation. I write. I find myself dissolved into these letters which you hold in your hands.

WHEN YOU GROW UP YOU WILL TRAVEL TO TALK—

In Bavaria, my talk about Canadian women's child sexual abuse narratives is greeted with silence. The sound of a hundred breaths inhaled. A woman asks ... *"How can it be that a professor would tell this story, so personal, so revealing. We never speak of this."*

At Sookmyung Women's University in Seoul, women nod their heads and say *"Yes. Yes, we don't speak of this...."* The affirmative—the imperative to tell the story is inhabited by the impossibility of its telling.

In Mysore, I am reminded of cross-cousin and uncle-niece marriages. I talk about how this cultural specificity of incest taboos complicates my impulse to misread. Nonetheless a man denounces me as cultural imperialist. How dare I bring these stories of abuse to contaminate his India. Throughout the room, Indian women from the north and south stand up to protest his silencing. After the talk, a professor from the Punjab introduces me to her thirteen-year-old daughter.

"I never travel without her," she explains, *"I do not trust my household."*

CHILDREN WHO HAVE BEEN ABUSED WILL TURN INWARD,

but there is something that will wake them, bring them back into a circle of humanity. And that is if the abuse to which they have been submitted is named and admitted to be true. And they long especially to have this abuse admitted to by the one who abused them. Yet, it is most common for a man who has raped a child to deny that the rape occurred, and to imply that the child made the story up, or if evidence is presented, to claim the child initiated the rape by seducing him. And these claims cause a second suffering as terrible as the first.

What one remembers is false
say critics who may be perpetrators
maybe not.
Critics say *memory lies*
With whom? she asks.

Perpetrators' denial (*no harm done*); rage (*just try and nail me*); hatred (she *drove me out of my right mind*); confusion (*what harm did I do?*); love (she *was always my special girl*); ignorance (*children have no memories before three*); shame (*how will I live with myself?*); *false* logic (how could I?) fear (*how will I live?*); self-delusion (*this too shall pass*).

Stories cannot be reconstructed without fear of denunciation or accusations of malice, lunacy or false memory. Looking over her shoulder, she imagines with hindsight and rehearses original loss. *Lost*—she repeats this word caught up in a story with too many familiar characters gone wrong. The pain of remembering is a revictimization of sorts.

MEMORY HOLDS HER UP TO LIGHT
AND SHAKES HER DOWN.

This small body returns.

(inside your ear
she sounds the moon
off course
howls
for the circuitry
of home)

See me in am?

4/5/4

Tattoo

Mistake tattoos for photographs!

Expose silvered flesh!

A photograph can certainly throw you off the scent. You will get nowhere, for instance, by taking a magnifying glass to get a closer look: you will only see patches of light and dark, an unreadable mesh of grains. The image yields nothing to that sort of scrutiny, it simply disappears.

ANNETTE KUHN

Art, like dermatology, is fundamentally about the concealment or display of stigmatization. The artist is someone who both makes a mark and is marked.

BARBARA MARIE STAFFORD

tattoo   *an inscription. to dedicate (a book) to another*

incest tattoo   the inscription of your desire which, knowing no boundaries, is dedicated to a recognition of a family resemblance

tattoo   *originally from "tap toe" "shut the tap" ...* a signal for closing the bars

incest tattoo   the sound of his feet on the floor returning home, having closed the bars

tattoo   *a signal sounded on a drum or bugle to call troops to quarters*

incest tattoo   she could only write with the clack clack clatter of the typewriter. smooth monitors provided no release.

tattoo   verb transitive *to mark (the skin) with a permanent pattern by puncturing it and inserting a pigment*

incest tattoo   needle-sharp images under the skin

tattoo   noun *the signal, the pattern ... "the marks thus made"*

incest tattoo   the self-blaming questions

tattoo   the tattoo is large enough to remove his touch from her skin. she tries exotic animals along her forearm. trunks and tails swing between her breasts. the supple limbs of marsupials and lithe snakes curl at her ankles. along the creases of her toes, fine life-lines of night animals make useful interventions in charcoal. the bracelet of

friendship carved in the north winds around her wrist,
disguising his grip. none of her menagerie escape.

incest tattoo   whose hand makes the marks? yours or mine?
whose hand flicks the switch of my desire?

tattoo   *"the marks thus made"*

incest tattoo   she has no memory of this. she's making it up.
it never happened. she doesn't remember. she'll get him
into trouble. it wasn't him. it was the other one. she's
lying. she's doing it for her own good. she'll get it in the
end. she's not to be trusted. it's her creative imagination.
she's unreliable. it's a conspiracy. there'll be trouble to pay.

tattoo   *by puncturing it and inserting a pigment*

incest tattoo   mirrors are of no use when Hollywood makes
the invisible man look attractive. father in his zoot suit
was just a figment of her imagination.

tattoo   the celebrity feminist author runs her large-ringed
fingers through a cropped cut and talks about sex. will
pleasure and empowerment follow us all the days of our
lives after we dare to accompany our bodies to the local
all-women tattoo parlour for a little clit ring, a little gold
fish cut into the shoulder? a tiny buttercup branded again
and again zig zags the length of your spine.

incest tattoo   *The blood looked very satisfactory. She took
the blade out of her razor and washed it. Neatly and very
lightly, she carved a little star. Experience must show, she
thought. She carved little stars shaped like A's on her arms,
and then she got up the courage to make curves. She did not*

cut deeply. She was not interested in hurting herself. On her breasts she made lovely arabesques, on her forearms almost unnoticeable cross-hatchings of little houses and trees. They did not show very much, but she knew they were there and was comforted.

tattoo   in love, the letter invades the flesh

incest tattoo   the letter is banished
the law invades
words flee or turn up
in the urgent shape of food lines,
claustrophobic pirouettes

tattoo   wholesome pointillism, skin deep

incest tattoo   the shape of his drowned body
his "jeweled coral head"
wet, hard, sharp, cutting

tattoo   *Welts, scars, cuts, tattoos, perforations, incisions, inlays, function quite literally to increase the surface space of the body.... They create not a map of the body, but the body precisely as a map.*

incest tattoo   an entrepreneurial feminist tattoo artist propagandizes about the virtues of her trade, the therapeutic character of her ornamented pain. the last scene of the film is tacked on without explanation. a naked woman stretches out on a table in a garage. a woman stands over her clothed in leather. they do not speak. a hollow thud sounds and elicits a small gasp or exhalation as the naked woman's torso jerks. (the camera pulls back) the leather-clad woman holding a hydraulic stapler comes into view.

as the woman on the table rises, her glazed eyes sink inside her head. upright, her breasts bleed from a dozen metal badges stapled to her chest. the women smile triumphant. the film ends.

tattoo   first she builds the house, a temporary shelter, just so she can remember the layout. the largest room visitors can enter is the father room. freshly wallpapered, the permanent pattern is of her own design. an image of the father, zoot-suited and serene, is multiplied over and over in her computer and then blown up 400% in a colour copier. she photographs herself in all the rooms. later she burns it to the ground.

incest tattoo   *a dying*

Put father where he belongs. In the rooms of the living. Or under the stairs. Or outside behind the garage in plain sight of any unseeing neighbours. Watch him crawl through the stairwells of my words as I write, quiet enough to startle you. Catch a glimpse of him, as he creeps across the ceiling, torso dangling, high-wire actor above your chair. Watch him spin a sticky thread long enough to lose your concentration.

In a blink, the blank membrane of your eyelid thickens into this dark wall you stare through. Through this exercise of paternal mnemonics, you remember nights of frail architecture where father or uncle, grandfather or brother await us in city block after city block of father rooms. This alleyway, littered with debris, fallen leaves (sing autumn) and the clatter of tin cans at your ankle leads up to a street named ... *No, no, not you* ... Street-corner lights of lurid neon or the flicker of a thousand candles project shadows twice the size of ordinary men, cocks flaccid between their legs, or hard and puny beneath distended bellies rippling with dinner rolls or the spice of curried haggis. In some rooms, fathers remember themselves, acknowledge the whereabouts of their hands, the ill-gotten gains called incest. Or they find deceptive routes and say nothing—leaving you long nights to disguise yourself as the narcoleptic vine that plays hide and seek like bedroom wallpaper.

Swing Memory
(a lesson in altitude)

To articulate the past historically ... means to seize hold of a memory ... as it flashes up at the moment of danger.

WALTER BENJAMIN

There is a pain—so utter—
It swallows substance up—
Then covers the Abyss with Trance—
So Memory can step
Around—across —upon it—
As one within a Swoon—
Goes safely—where an open eye—
Would drop Him—Bone by Bone.

EMILY DICKINSON

Trauma ... is always the story of a wound that cries out, that addresses us in the attempt to tell us of a reality or truth that is not otherwise available. This truth, in its delayed appearance and its belated address, cannot be linked only to what is known, but also to what remains unknown in our very actions and our language.

CATHY CARUTH

Push me
some more
Daddy.
My 2nd mall

X 0976

MY FATHER WRITES ON THE BACK OF MY PHOTOGRAPH:

push me some more Daddy

I swing therefore I am. The soles of my feet stretch flat out towards the lens. My hands tighten around these ropes. A gap-toothed smile glints below bobbed hair. Rows of fuzzy trees disappear, a tree trunk blurs to the left. He pushes me away to where the swing disappears in green. A moment later, I return, descending toward his camera's eye. The shutter snaps us to attention. I smile therefore I am. I laugh inside out loud.

We celebrate my third birthday.

The back and forth motion on the swing makes me heady with pleasure. Hot summer air blows up my red skirt; the wet white triangle blinks with pleasure; hot thrills with a giggle. At the top, delight squeals through my teeth. Ropes loosen in my hands; grip tighter, suspended, I wake up *en air*. (In the language, I loves to hear.) *Dans la lune* (I thinks she is saying.) For this brief moment, her grip slackens, hands slide upwards. To fall would not be such a long route home. A sudden jerk and fingers grip in fear. I remembers. Her eyes return to his long look.

One day I remembers; the next, I regrets—*shame shame go away.* Swing the back and forth record of memory's denial: blame, no blame. *Shame shame go away.* The stutter: lips call up small words, the ache of I alive again. How can I carry this girl home? How I shifts. My mirrored look blurs then once again reaffirms, I vision. I wants you to know her small i sits in this knowledge others remember. Small children, fingers sticky with candy or come, chart and gather a future in these words *I remember.*

(Swing is a longer word than pain. Marked by flight, flesh slides along the roof. The slick sounds our tongue makes as though words could caress us through sleep.)

Grownups sit on swings when we're lonesome or in love. Sometimes we kiss each other from so high up, we can barely reach. Her lover will not make love. Furious, filled up with rage, I demands attention. He gives it to her in his glance from the other side of the moon. Outside, ice clouds scud over the city, erase the tops of buildings. *Hold onto your head.* It too might disappear. Suspended in this strange loop of desire, our feet barely touch down but we're off again, defying what it is that keeps us so near the ground. To tunnel through each other's longing, we let go our grip.

On this morning forty years later, my step falters in *a crisis of reminiscences.* A dream zone opens and I am stranded in an image blizzard, a white-out world which crashes in. I cry, *Push me higher daddy. Push me.* He says *push me.* The voice echoes interior *in terror.* A wind's hair breath in my ear from far away. He comes close enough. *(I cannot see his face.)*

I am fanned by the wings of memory.

THE NUB OF THE RIDDLE

> *An unused memory gets lost, ceases to exist, dissolves into nothing—an alarming thought. Consequently, the faculty to preserve, to remember, must be developed. Before your inner eye, ghostly arms emerge, groping about in a dense fog aimlessly.*

Yes was also one of her words. At first she said *no*. Then she learned how to talk and the word *no* was not enough to protect her from her longing. Her *longing*, she said. When his touches stopped, she was angry her livelong day.

The first time I makes love, her body splits apart into flesh with fluids for pleasure, gasping for air, heaving her inside out through her mouth. The other part stops breathing. I told herself *don't be stupid, it's just breathing and sex* until he picks her blueness up in his arms and carries her (naked, not breathing) to the car, top down, a chill air between her and the vinyl seat, a shock to her breath. Inhaling the pink, just in time to avoid public knowledge and certain humiliation.

(When she remembers to tell her story in the middle of a different love, she hears, *Sometimes, the first time, girls can't breathe. Their tongues remember their mouths filled up.*)

> *Here and here alone do we have the nub of the riddle of the "leap into the organic." How can we understand that a thought, which is initially psychical, becomes a physiological mechanism without ceasing to be a thought?*

initially psychical? A curtsey appeared as a depression marked by her skirt. As soon as he jammed his cock in her mouth, she was upwardly mobile, gaining altitude. Or at least that's how it feels from here. Looking back from this vantage point, her white dress and socks merged with a ceiling pattern. Warm air rises like bread between her legs. Spine tingling breath at the nape of her neck spreads heat. Her body wears arousal like a hat, red and tasseled above her fuzzy head that abandons her or escapes into what comes next.

(This altitude was nothing but narrative distance wrote two women, one looking down at the other on the beach, understanding how each of them required a speaker to maintain her voice in time.)

> *A woman's memory then. Unwinding back to double-sided images: "truth" plus fiction.*

Her analyst says it doesn't matter whether her memories are fantastic or real: the trauma remains. Treat it as real. As real as she can remember. Freud coined the terms of unconscious paradox and contradiction. Phantasms and the real are weak oppositions.

The spill over of this memory work begins at this moment on July 24, 1991: *If there is no difference, then why bother remembering,* she thinks. Though this is not a question of will. The remembering, a "leaking through"; her mind, a permeable membrane haunted by another time, an unspoken history.

> *(There is something about the body of the other that the hysteric cannot "take," cannot swallow, inhale or touch, according to circumstances.)*

First we remember the sounds, the smells, the single image flash arrested. Criminal injuries recorded. She coughs and coughs 'til her head falls off.

> *He goes on to look for yet another moment that would bring them into play, for he is hard put to see why it should have been a smell, and that particular smell, if it had nothing to do with the conflict, that became the mark, the scar, of the conflict.*

It came back. Her body's stories revisit. Revisited? One day, remembering, she soils her pants, infantalized into forgetting she is not a child. Were these memories to uncover or collect? Is this archeology, or hunting and gathering? She needs to know patterns of brains and biology.

The displacement of sensations … as though part of me is vacant, the other, knowing and watchful, tends the shop, protecting survival at all costs. The cost is apparently this pattern of disembodied drift. A hard forgetting. Am I writing this or is it writing me? The body disturbed beyond its own belief—no controlled distance between mental patterns and physical sensations.

At lunch with the sound composer, she retells the story of a poem "Listen." A man and a woman are in a kitchen. The man reads an anthropological account of a round dance that celebrates community; the woman makes a salad. Greens stain red as she grates her fingers to the bone. She finishes retelling the story in the middle of the cafeteria and she coughs and coughs with the composer, laughing about castration. She coughs and she coughs and remembers touching her father's come.

TRY HYPNOSIS:

the fine line between weightless monologue and conversation stretches like longing before me. I sit in impatient anticipation, waiting, less for something to happen than for a clear vision, sudden epiphany, or a reasonable facsimile of truth. A bad attitude. My footsteps and the space inside are already inhabited by dream—a zone where history meets me at least *halfway*, according to Freud, who described how in his own first studies of hysteria, *before they come for analysis, the patients know nothing about these scenes.* Freud's first analysis was terminated by Dora. Did she refuse to "know nothing"?

Hypnotized, I see his hands, his face.

Battling memory's prohibitions, I remember. Not at any other time, do I identify him as *father* except in my dreams and waking fear. To the count of numbers repeated backwards, I hear my voice, soft with easeful care. I walk down the hill towards the willow trees behind my childhood home …

10 …
9 …

Had she remembered then what he had done to her? She would learn to hate him again, take him again to her bitter centre, turn him this way and that in her loathing. Injuries would be examined, large and small. With her tongue pressing him away from her, she would eat him like the sea. Her throat will spew forth his body, tanned and sometimes beautiful.

8 …
7 …

My body limp with fatigue. semi-somnambulent she/i begins to remember (or reconstruct?) As her/my body grows limp, my hand rests on an imaginary video camera to record the scene that will unfold. (*Which scene? And why?*) As my mind slips back through time (or rummages through the bin of the present moment?) his image rushes towards me with all the terrible lucidity of what? the truth? or some imaginary correspondence which recounts a story I can only now bear to hear. I tell the story about the father room.

6 ...
5 ...

How To Remember:

> *In the mind one forms the image of a three-dimensional space, a well-furnished house or even an entire city. Do you wish to remember that printing was invented in 1436? Then place a book in the thirty-sixth memory place in the fourth room of the first house in town.*

Put father where he belongs. In the bedroom. Or under the stairs. Or outside behind the garage in plain sight of any unseeing neighbours. Watch him crawl through the stairwells of my words as I write ...

4 ...
3 ...

An abandoned wood-framed lodge with many bedrooms. I am on holiday with my parents at a Lake Muskoka borrowed cottage. My mother and father suntan naked on the rocks. At 12, I'm not unfamiliar with my parent's nakedness, but uncomfortable with my own feelings of vulnerability. Am I to remove my clothes too? Does this freedom from clothing mean we are all happy under our skins. My father's penis curls like a fiddlehead between his thighs. What does his intent look at me mean? My father's penis curls like a snake beneath his belly. Playfully, he laughs at my discomfort as I disappear between the rocks and trees.

When I look into the imaginary frame of this moment, I see the mirrored and fogged over image of the girl's exhalations as she runs as fast as her legs will carry her through the forest.

How do I remember my discomfort? Am I fearful of other moments of nakedness and vulnerability? Is this simply adolescent prudery and newfound self-conscious sexual awareness? Or is my flight a response to child sexual abuse?

Did father die twice for me?

Once when he drowned himself.

Twice, when I killed him, remembering.

2 ...

1 ...

THERE ARE MANY THINGS WE KNOW . . .

> *... but which we are not supposed to know. Sometimes there is a conspiracy to silence us. But, at other times, it may be that what we have to tell is something no one wants to know because what we say does not fit into the scheme of things as they are understood to be.*

Today my mother gasped when I told her my waking dream. My head snapped back. "Whiplash," I said. And my mouth open so wide it hurt. *Yes,* I said, *it hurt. My head snapped back until he held it here with his hands so I couldn't breathe with it in my mouth.* "I smell rye and Kools," I say. (I am almost a baby.)

When I looks at the photographs of myself as a child, the mouth looks smaller than I could ever have imagined.—the force of impact whips her neck into a frenzy of stitched pain. Her head locked into place looked neither right or left. Straight ahead, she thought. Think "straight ahead" and things will return to how they were yesterday, before she saw his drunken pleasure.

I looks at the photographs imagining her neck hurts. Her mouth is too wide.... I/she cannot cry like this. Her/my mouth opens and out comes the story as gesture. Her/my shoulders propelled back into the chair, slap of the body, mouth open now, her lungs collapse, squeeze air into him, his penis so big it burst her body. Her body all the time pulsating, her voiceless throat not quite singing. Is this memory or a life inside the body moving out? Story communicable now, perceived, apprehended somewhere between her shoulders stiff now remembering, her hands, hair wet, the pain, tears enough.

Afterwards she knows part of the pain is her love for him, the feel of his hands all over. Afterwards she remembers she hates the smell of rye whiskey. His smell. His uncaring abandonment to his own pleasure.

The waking dream: denial

I'm making it up. Imagining it. She imagines her lover will abandon her. *Why?* he asks. She is a wound, sliced thin and bleeding. She is damaged and will not heal.

The waking dream: evidence

Why would the mother in her dream stand and look away if she knew he was mad and harming her daughter?

Her mother is coming to visit her and she is afraid to offend her. How does she say to her that my father, her husband abused her once and perhaps again. She can't remember. How can she stop her mother from familial denial of her own story or the explanation of her status as good mother as though this were the whole issue. She, the issue, will speak of this now.

The first time I tell my mother I remember my father pushing his cock into my mouth, she bursts into tears, rocking, rocking, back and forth in her chair. *He did that to me too,* she says. And she cries, moaning *my god, my god.*

In response, my mother cries out her heart and wails, *Oh my god Jan. He did that to me too. He used to hold my head until I thought I would suffocate all our married life. My body was like meat. Was meat. He never touched me with affection or love. He*

grabbed my breasts. He grabbed my crotch. I am still humiliated
and shamed by my submission, my passivity, my ...

The waking dream: denial

(The first time I wrote outside of school as a child, I thought
I had nothing to say. I had nothing to say but scribbled notes
to god, edges of the page scorched with stolen matches, then
rolled and rolled into small scrolls. Imagining myself burying
mysterious treasure or leaving enigmatic clues to future gen-
erations, I stuffed these small offerings in the cracks in the
ceiling where they disappeared ... *oh god oh god oh god?* Who
found these unbelieving words calling over and over?)

> *Explore your hunches but don't write about it.*
> *The relations will be distressed and upset. Yes you are*
> *remembering.*

Or:

> *Perhaps ... yes, you are remembering. I can't imagine*
> *him doing this to you.... but perhaps he did ... This is*
> *your story to explore.... All I can say is don't write*
> *about it. All I can say is I didn't abuse you.*

The waking dream: evidence

At a literary gathering, I meet a novelist who writes about the
dissociation experienced by a girl who would be my age were
she not a fictive character. *Even* Scientific American *has some-*
thing to say about child sexual abuse and memory, she says as
she directs me to a study of the brain:

> *We are unable to remember traumatic events that take place early in life because the hippocampus has not yet matured to the point of forming consciously accessible memories. The emotional memory system, which may develop earlier, clearly forms and stores its unconscious memories of these events. And for this reason, the trauma may affect mental and behavioural functions in later life, albeit through processes that remain inaccessible to consciousness.*

The waking dream: denial

She reads it everywhere. In a postcard titled "Snake Club, Sarasota Florida, 1944," a row of pubescent children sit along the soda bar caressing their snakes. One girl sucks a popsicle suggestively. Or is she merely sucking? Is this "merely" in a world where to suck means nipple or cock? The soda jerk smiles into his faucet.

The image is edgy, fishy, ambiguous, unsettling, fascinating: as mesmerizing and hypnotic as we imagine the snakes to be.

The waking dream: evidence

She hears voices: *You're making it up. The two of you. You're out to get him.*

The waking dream: denial

I ask my mother how old I was when the nightmares began.
Four or five.
And the convulsions?
Several when you were four or five ...

The waking dream: evidence

Writing is a very good way to get myself out of the blues.
The patter of fingertips while munching stuffed grape leaves
and lemon, chopped. Chunks of citrus membrane exceed
despair in their sourness.

The waking dream: denial

This memory process leaves me incapacitated at times ... not
so much depressed, but distracted, dissociative. All day long,
my body limps along behind me, trying to catch up to my
thoughts, losing keys, my purse, forgetting my wallet. I am,
as they say "an absent-minded professor," a good enough
explanation as I muster along, missing appointments, dead-
lines, sometimes unable to move from my desk to the door,
utterly immobilized by the thought my father molested me.
The more I think about it, the more my life appears retro-
spectively ordered by his disorder—as though each moment,
gesture, conversation, lover, accomplishment, or decision
reverberates from the shock waves of incest.

A part of me is on time while another sneaks into the back

row late. The former is on vacation so she misses almost everything. The therapist says *the child in you is crying out.*

Fine, I say, *cry out, cry rivers, but cry on your own time. Leave me mine.*

Will I become a bitter old woman? Bitter, ungenerous, uncompromising—half my mind blasted history, bombed out of my senses, the other half foraging for what I needs, hoarding all—kisses, champagne, lampposts.

Be understanding but not indulgent, she chides herself. *Keep yourself to yourself and calculate what has been lost.*

The waking dream: denial

Now I'm less certain of the cock's identity. Less willing to lay blame. Less eager to name him. Worried about whom? More concerned about now. What is accomplished in this memory and the tension between truth and not knowing? What is it I speaks? The taut jaw clench of uncertainty guiding me into and through this thicket familiar to so many. So difficult to speak. How do I write the accretion of sickening details. A story that spells out the facts without doubt is a story of dread. The dread of the author who confesses her history, risking misreadings by those who don't believe her or wish for silence. Will her story vanish?

The waking dream: evidence

As a child, I escape into narratives of my own. Not quite fantasy, but fantastic readings of other's stories. I can split into the main character and her mother, or the mother of her best friend and the best friend's boyfriend, the sculptor and the statue. I read my way into two places at once, all the while remembering how to put myself back together at a moment's notice. In the dream, I open a freezer to find a forest of glistening herbs, their fragrances frozen like my body.

The waking dream: denial

For a few years, the only place I feel safe is living on an island. At the Salt Spring Island workshop, we are asked to reimagine ourselves. Make up what we feel we've lost. Drawing a large full-size figure of myself, I give myself a huge single-eye head ribbed with web-like scales. This writing eye/I suspended over a neck the texture of barbed wire, a Victorian collar so painfully tight it keeps the head/writing-I afloat no matter the storm. Torso, slippery green frog skin, a body to slide through watery places. Spine, molten thread of crimson breath escapes through vaginal lips—furious, speechless fire. The right foot on this body, no more than an amputated stump, imagines itself "pinned down," a child caught writhing.

The right foot remembers what is lost. This phantom limb sprouts wings.

The waking dream: evidence

Later at the Ganges market on Salt Spring Island where I stop to have coffee and write, a woman, a stranger, asks me what I am writing and I tell her this story.

My disclosure triggers memories of her own sexual abuse. *Sometimes*, she says, *my whole body convulses.*

As she speaks, her arms swing wild in front of her. She remembers *in spite of herself.*

The waking dream: denial

A likely crybaby story:

> There may also be a thoroughly illogical element ... namely the recent popularity, among middle-class people who can afford therapists, of seeing oneself as victim. In conversation one African-American psychiatrist unkindly called this me-tooism; at a time when consciousness is being raised about real oppression, the confused and depressed take comfort in saying, "Me too."

Real oppression? Me too.

Doesn't this minimize the points of common cause we can find between children across cultures? Is it an accident that at the moment some white women are afforded privilege in a racially unequal culture, our tales of childhood abjection elevate us to the podium of grief—maligned, wounded, and in need of healing. Is it an accident that at this moment when the turntable is spun to different rhythms, the white feminist is accused of hogging the floor, stealing the limelight, kissing the tail of the master.

We cannot compare pain. We must not cry foul fakery or fraud. We do not feign injury or play dead. In these stories of abuse, how do we come to terms with what is lost when we too eagerly ignore any child's voice of injury and abandonment? What is found in the attentive gap between compassionate listening and self-reflection?

The waking dream: evidence

Without witnesses, my historical "truth" eludes me; memory is suspect, a contrivance. This writing is not propelled by a desire to lie or misrepresent—and yet, how do I take into account the constructedness of memory itself?

The waking dream: denial

The historical truth of a woman writer's life lies in the reader's grasp of her intratext: the body of her writing and not the writing of her body.

The waking dream: evidence

In my circumstances, is the fictive my only alternative to silence and repression? The filmmaker Claude Lanzmann writes: *Fiction is a transgression. I deeply believe there are some things that cannot and should not be represented.* He writes this about the Holocaust and some find it possible to appropriate this trauma of ethnic cleansing for the stories of child sexual abuse—the secret pleasure through torture of children by adults. But the "secret holocaust" is a facile comparison. Each trauma resonates with the perverse banality of everyday destruction, one doesn't feel the burning flesh and cannot compare the pain.

And yet there are parallels in the way "normal" behaviour can organize itself so carefully to accommodate anguish and inhumanity. The man who spent his orphaned childhood in a Nazi camp writes about his life after the Allied "liberation."

Like so many abused children, he was told *You must forget it all … the way you forget a bad dream.* As a result, his sense of ominous dread and mistrust did not end: *Nobody ever told me the war was over…. The good life is but a trap. The camp's still there—just hidden and well disguised. They've taken off their uniforms and dressed themselves up in nice clothes so as not to be recognized.*

How do we measure this loss? *The torture of children by adults.*

The child wants to write a different ending, but can't find her pencil to begin.

The daily insists on mistrust; small betrayals. Thoughts of suicide or madness write themselves in commonplace books of bad advice. Her fears and dislocations may be dismissed as neurosis. Or will the ending be less tortuous?

The waking dream: denial

An Ontario based survey based on almost 10,000 respondents … found that 1 in 8 girls (and 1 in 23 boys) suffer sexual abuse. More narrowly framed than previous studies that included verbal taunting and sexual comments, one in eight female respondents indicated than an adult had either: 1. exposed themselves to the child more than once, 2. threatened to have sex with the child, 3. touched the child on sexual parts of the body, 4. tried to have sex with the child, or 5. had had sex with the child….

The inescapable conclusion … is that one in eight girls growing up in Canada today will likely be a victim of serious sexual abuse, that the perpetrator will in all likelihood be male, usually a male known to the victim and in some position of authority over the victim.... The dramatic extent of the sexual abuse of female children in families has been further corroborated by the recent Women's Safety Project in which a random representative sample of 420 Toronto women (ages 18 to 64) were interviewed in depth about their experience of sexual and physical assault. In this study, 17 percent (or one woman in six) reported at least one experience of incest before age 16.

The waking dream: evidence

You remember your own best friend. Sunday at aunt C's and everyone is in the living room except M (age 13) and my father (age 37). A while later M turns up looking wary, her eyes fluttering back and forth.

Looking for me? I ask in a whisper.

Yes, she says, *he touched me* here, pointing to her new breasts, trembling wet in her bathing suit. Shaking, I say to mother, *he touched her* there.

Mother looks upset as she leaves the room. Father gets into trouble. *M isn't a woman but a girl*, shouts mother.

M says, *my father abused me too.*

I thought it must be a matter of M's breasts. Mature for her age, M looked *like a woman*. (This could have developed into a scandal, the drama of the event, a tip off. But no one identified the iceberg.)

The waking dream: denial

The scene is not merely "smoothed and polished and painted over," as happens in all memory of important events.... Having recalled a scene, you begin to paint it, using the palette of the generic but retroactive description that came with the first intimations of memory.... In real life the tighter the chain of causation ... —the better the narrative.

The waking dream: evidence

Fear travels intergenerationally. Fear travels in dreams. Father lays himself down in bed under a neon sign blinking "Gentle Man." He is her perimeter, her peripheral vision.

The waking dream: denial

Innocence is not a property of childhood but a portion of adult desire.... If there is wide-spread sexual abuse of children, then it is not so much the innocence of childhood as the boundary between adult and child, their status as stable and knowable entities, which starts to shake. Child abuse confronts us wfith the violence of limits flouted and transgressed. Bodies open where they should remain closed, and a defining space is invaded— the space which conceptually as well as physically is meant to keep children and adults apart.

The waking dream: evidence

At the lecture, the artist projects slides about surveillance and the history of the camera obscura, the nineteenth-century precursor to the photograph and cinema. In the darkened room, the world we survey is liquid green and gorgeous. Early in the century, the author of *Peter Pan* donated a camera obscura building to his hometown along with a playground for children. Standing in the dark interior room, the playground is reflected through a window and refracted by a roof mirror onto a horizontal white table. The image, a utopian disk of innocence catches a circular icon of bodies and swings. I can hear the children's pleasure in the smudge of a girl's dress in the image. *Push me higher,* she cries.

The waking dream: denial

If my memories were confined to an intermediate space of consciousness where inhibitions seem to be put on hold, I might be entirely sceptical, but this is not the case. Nor is it the case with others I know.

C's memories haunted her for years and she eventually wrote them down as a series of terrifying drawings of a baby thrust up against the corner of a basement wall. Tormented by the possibility of a father's betrayal, she marshalled her courage, eventually confessing her suspicious feelings to her younger sisters. Two of them confirmed her accusations, revealing that they too had been molested. The fourth sister refused to believe anyone.

The waking dream: evidence

A. and I met on the beach. She could do cartwheels. I managed arabesques. I was 12 or perhaps 11; A, a year younger. Two years later we found ourselves bused into the same school together. The two of us would become best friends.

A, a pianist, eventually became a champion chess player; at this point in her dexterous development, her fingers could move across the keyboard with the brilliant strategic speed of her brain. Her mind like mine, filled with mischief. We got into trouble for saying "Shit!" on missing the championship long-jump (A.) or wandering away during a late-night astronomy session in the country with the class (A. & I). Exploring the woods behind Fairport Beach School, we disappeared from sight. Our teacher, Mr. P., a suspicious and pinched, though challenging man, became certain the two of us were impregnating ourselves with several of the boys in the class and set up spontaneous search parties. Meanwhile under the moonlight, we remained disinterested in any of the boys in our class—immature, inarticulate, inane! Instead, we talked about the stars immediately above us and wandered through the mysterious hollows of the woods. We loved each other on this slouch of land as it opened out into the blank shimmer of Lake Ontario—best friends and all that entailed: lifelong affection, absolute trust, raucous laughter, ecstatic unfathomable pleasures in our conversations.

For 30 years, A. couldn't tell me that my father molested her.

The waking dream: denial

Work and its "work" (or work and its object, its artifact) are the names that are given to the pain and the imagination as they begin to move from being a self-contained loop within the body to becoming the equivalent loop now projected into the external world. It is through this movement out into the world that the extreme privacy of the occurrence (both pain and imagining are invisible to anyone outside the boundaries of the person's body) begins to be sharable, that sentience becomes social and thus acquires its distinctly human form.

The waking dream: evidence

A's fingers move with the brilliant speed of her brain. One afternoon on the piano bench in the living room, her small strong body plays Chopin or something that makes me pirouette around the room and leap through the dining room in turned out balletic style. Something happened. I noticed out of the corner of my eye or perhaps not. Maybe I had gone to let the dog in or walked to the kitchen for something to drink. We were 13 or maybe close to 14. Though it wouldn't be until I disclosed my sexual abuse memories that A. would tell me on the telephone how my father molested her on the piano bench and how she kept silent but feared him the rest of his life.

The waking dream: denial

When she suddenly remembers being molested by her father, a young woman refuses to let him visit her children. When her father denies everything, she is marginalized as "hysterical," a crisis that splits the family asunder. A year after the first accusations, another family member meets a former childhood neighbour of the family. On hearing of the turmoil, the woman bursts into tears, confessing the accused father now grandfather molested her many times as a child when she was too afraid to tell.

Or the artist who works all her life for social justice only to discover that her son has been molested by her father, a man of "honour" and leader at the centre of a large respectful community. Her long-revered father refuses to believe he has harmed the young men. Nor can he believe he has not. To complicate matters, the artist cannot explain her lifelong inability to experience sexual pleasure. She cannot bring herself to ask her father the truth and consoles herself with his silence.

As she nurses him through his long painful death, they will not speak of this.

The waking dream: evidence

The notes falter for a moment, but remain almost flawless in memory. The piano continues to play.

Pumps

Melancholy persons are foreigners in their maternal tongue.
JULIA KRISTEVA

> *mother's shoes her pumps*
> *heels helicopter through grass*
> *spinning out calves*
> *her ankle*

Well ... the biggest house in the country rises out of a child's rural phantasm: foundation, a barn—chicken tracks on the patio lead to the pool, now buried. Twenty years later, she will look for her childhood house. The space mother might have worn through had the linoleum not been torn up to change the colour scheme. From this point in time, not much has moved except the bulldozer, arrested in its crash through her bedroom wall.

The machine waits for Monday morning when it will take down the house and make way for a new shopping centre that won't be built. Instead Valley Farm Road will end here at the highway on its way to a new housing complex replacing the drive-in movie theatre she watched as a child through the bedroom window, located in the bedroom wall now blasted open in this mechanical shower of stucco and memory, glass and recollection.

This moment of destruction and change suspends her inside a Sunday afternoon drive to revisit her childhood home. In what was once countryside, she is frightened by this machine. Frightened by how this machine could rock through her bedroom door, lurch noisily through her books, her untidy desk, right into and over these rumpled bed-clothes. The window could open like this and no questions asked with the crash and creak of wooden timbers. Window panes fall into her hands, her eyes. She can't really see any of this. She remembers none of it. She only knows that this bull-dozer stands between her former broadloom and the lawn outside waiting for the workmen to return to finish the job.

In a few years, there will be no trace of this moment, the residue of building, tracks of machines. Only a few bushes, brief memory of the pond, pummeled into this new shape; the course of a creek whipped into new hills and ravines. Willow trees tipped into themselves, tossed uprooted onto the new curve of land. Bending down she might trace the outline of an archeological site, a newly suburban dig. Just here she could track the concrete line of the patio. Digging down with a stick, a patch of aqua plaster breaks loose into her hand. She traces the geometric line of the swimming pool, drowned and buried like her father by the years. The Indian ruins a few miles north had been a special treat for her to visit as a child; now her own childhood home is a settler's hidden treasure. Buried, a sacred bowl of bourgeois rural life rolled into this patch of land by the highway, looking out towards another highway, lying low beside the nuclear power lines cut through the apple orchard. Waiting for some well-trained archeologist to find where she walked through what remained of Aunt Peggy's lilac trees and cut a bouquet to remember the scent of her mother.

In the movie *Serial Mom*, the mother's obsessions are made parodically dangerous when Kathleen Turner murders Patricia Hearst because she wears white shoes after Labour Day. This is the world of my mother. Of rites and shoes. Of fashion and life terms. Or rather this was my mother's world. This is the mother of my childhood. The woman who birthed me at 22. By the age of 43, my age as I write these words, my mother had witnessed the dissolution of her marriage, the loss of another daughter in childbirth, the death of her father, the strokes and recovery of her mother, the suicide of her husband, and the loss of herself to mind-numbing despair and anguish.

Every Tuesday and Saturday, her mother drove her to the Gladys Gayle School of Dance at the Ajax shopping centre. From the time she was 5 until she was 16, she danced and could feel her spirit, or something she imagined to be her spirit—something unlike Sunday School—well up in her. Jesus didn't do for her what a day of ballet or tap and chips and gravy did. She remembers the tingling surge of heat, the light-bodied smile of a good routine, a lively performance. The moves, the steps, the hand movements were recorded here in her fingers when they tapped out dance music, Chopin, or something wild and Hungarian.

The tempo of piano or cello or full-blown orchestra could choreograph her childhood body in small discrete gestures which create a callous on the outside of her index finger. Her dancing body still pirouettes in her fingertips, rubbing secret messages into her skin.

Beside the telephone, her mother's fields of four-leaf clovers would bloom after long conversations. The loops swirled and multiplied as talk became more involved with traces, a hopeful whirlpool of pencil-grey doodles. Laughter or tense listening or sorrow. Four-leaf clovers: my mother's luck circling through.

The little girl loved her mother so she could not sleep. Sleepless with the love of her mother, she tried to please, but then she couldn't. She knew her mother would be lost without her. She would stay close enough to be heard at all times. She tagged along everywhere. Tried to please. To be the very best tap dancer in the IGA. Most agile ballerina in the forest of shoppers at the Sherwood Mall. Best tree climber in the orchard.

The mother's story doesn't begin with a coat hanger, a skein of wool, a tall slender woman like an opera singer. It goes somewhere. She learns to knit.

Crying out, thrown from bed by her husband, she crawls to bed with her own little girl ... for protection. Ellipses mark the chasm of mother/daughter years in another night's hurried footsteps. (The writer sticks her finger in her ear to stop memory's whirl. What did the girl-I think feel in the comfort of her mother's sorrow? Her mother's arms enfold her close in the spoon of her Need. Upper-case. Not queen-for-a-day, but mother-for-life. For comfort, there was this warmth and the knowledge of the man father, bitten with rage because *your brains are all in your boobs,* he told her.

Like it or not, breasts were not mine, not yet. At night I copied and altered my mother's body on the sewing machine, stitching together "woman" in white linen, armholes squared like *Vogue Magazine,* colourless as a bride.

In her later life, my mother would renew herself. But much earlier, I wanted to mother her into being. Enmeshed with her pain, as a young girl, I grieved, rebelled and ran away, creeping back into her arms for comfort which I would then refuse.

In 1947, my father will not accompany my mother to Winnipeg for her abortion. My mother will never forgive him but two years later, they will marry. She *had to*; he fathered her first pregnancy. I am the first born, in Brandon. We move west. Life is not easy in the mountains. We move east itching for a break. In 1955, a second daughter will die after three days from birth defects. My mother is advised not to look at the child. She will never hold the child. She will not name the child.

For decades, my mother mourns this baby's death. *A punishment for my abortion*, she says. Yet she marches with me on pro-choice rallies. *We need to change the world and my guilt,* she says.

While mother births my sister, I sleep in Daddy's bed every night. *Mummy! Mummy! Where's the baby* I cry when she arrives home.

Mother collapses into Daddy's arms.
What have I done?

He says, *How can you trust anyone who bleeds for a month and then refuses to die.*

Father takes over the room just like this; narrative shifting dream caught midstream and damned if it doesn't trickle down this hillside. His cab chits found on the floor claim he had come from somewhere other than where he had come from. Niagara Falls. This deception didn't make sense except as an explanation for his libidinal desire. His voice, a liar's echo, too loud and thick with charm. (He knew she loved him.) The little I knew of him wrapped in some Canadian dream of mid-size splendour, tempered happiness.

She says: *It's day, everything is about to begin, except you, you never begin.*

This is not an unusual story. Mother drifts with ease into bitter dependence. Before marriage, she works as her future husband's secretary. On marrying, she gains a spouse but loses her job. In 1953, after a separation, she returns to her husband for another decade. When she throws him out, she can't refuse his return. Demoralized and too frightened by his temper, she doesn't walk out the door for another seven years.

[In this paragraph, she wants to take the mother's side, the side that is most familiar.] At 12, I hear a woman calling in the middle of the night to tell my mother she wants her husband. My mother is angry at the caller and slams the telephone down. The next morning, my mother will confide on the phone to her friend about leaving Daddy: *Miserable coot. Miserable coot*, she will call him. *The boys*, my brothers, are to go with her, *too young to be on their own*. I will be sent away with my father, she says as though concerned about my welfare.

I/she stood at the door listening to this conversation uncertain whether I/she was supposed to be in or out of the room. Uncertain whether I/she is/am separate or almost on my own. *Am I in a house or my home? Will I grow up "Daddy's girl"*—Daddy so scary, so full of life he plays "Stardust" or that "Girl from Ipanema" or songs about apples on cue. Or songs like horror movies make me squirm with something too close for comfort. Or the smash sound of the bathroom door mirror he accomplished one Sunday morning after she left church *on her way to hell.* Or the cracking sound her wrist makes at six years, when he tosses her in the air to fly. Crashing angel. Broken.

The look of the wounded woman when she knows the other is about to suffer something familiar. The look of defeat. Or someone who imagines these are the ropes to spin through.

If I did not agree to lose mother, I could not imagine or name her.

Wait for the word *mother* to rouse me from irritation or discomfort or procrastination or simply not writing. Not for mother. Gail calls her "gothic mother," veiled source of resistance *and* submission. Sometimes the comfort of her mirrored corridor refracts in an unforgiving sleight of hand. Resistance thickens in this place cried out as child.

Mother tells me one of her truths when I am grown up and 38. She says she wishes her daughter had been retarded. She turns to me and says she wishes I had been "retarded." She says she is relieved I am childless and *barren. It is easier this way.* She says she believes she—the mother—is an *infection.* She believes a hazardous epidemic will be reproduced through her children and her children's children.
It would be easier if you were retarded. You don't deserve a child. Already I have too much: a house, a car, a job.
What do you need with a child?

Tomorrow we will meet in mother's hotel room. Mother will weep saying, *I forgot I loved you so much. We grew so distant.*

Cuddle up a little closer, closer still and repeat after me.... And sometimes I could only pull back to disentangle myself from this love, to find a new wardrobe of feelings where I could do up my own buttons and find my own rhythm. In this new dance, there could be no betrayals.

The way to leave sadness is not necessarily by the road to success. Try a lover, a beloved pet, a house…. (She wrote "house" first, then erased it, not wanting to be perceived a vulgar materialist. Did this not explain why she found herself in her own house alone without the voices of parents who loathed each other?)

It wasn't that her house was her mother. It's just that it reminded her so much of her mother that she couldn't think "house" without her voice coming into the picture. This soft voice which spoke to her while she pinned a new dress for a special day. Or a hard voice that caught her reading in the middle of the night when she shouldn't. The midnight voice that interrupted Nancy Drew or *The Agony and the Ecstasy* or even Winston Churchill. The sound of this voice made her remember Cherry Ames' dress size and the smell of a tree in *Freckles*. Unsheltered, but not houseless, she listens for any forest bed. The hollow sound of marshes.

When she goes to the ocean to heal herself in the tilted world of the island, she finds a fish-bone carving of a bird and brings it to her mother who, like her, is yearning to fly.

The Father Room

That is a Dead Father, Thomas told them.
The children hugged each other tightly.
He doesn't look dead to us, said the girl.
He is walking, said the boy, Or standing up, anyhow.
He is dead only in a sense, Thomas said.
The children kissed each other, on the lips.

DONALD BARTHELME

You do not distinguish the boulder that buries you
beneath it, but only the force of the impact; so my pain
at the loss of everything I had called "father" was
threatening to crush me with its weight.

CHRISTA WOLF

The disaster is related to forgetfulness—forgetfulness
without memory, the motionless retreat of what has not
been treated.... To remember forgetfully: again, the
outside.

MAURICE BLANCHOT

My best client
I look healthy

May 23/54

FATHER APPEARED MONSTROUS TO SOME.

If I hated him, would it be easier? It was easier when I hated him. I hated him and he could do no right. A humiliation, a damnation, a shame and a rage—he moved inside the centre of my being. Dead, he is made monstrous—that ambiguous two-headed beast of a word meaning an *incredible marvel* and what *warns* and *predicts*.

Sometimes he was marvellous; occasionally a monster. Often he drove a convertible, white roof open to the summer sky. The seats always smelled of cigarettes. Sometimes of come. The back seat smokes, sings schmaltzy love songs. His hand smoothes the curve of her shoulder, performing a cha cha, or tonight, the samba. Hips swivel on command to the tune of any patio's rye and Coke.

FATHER APPEARED MARVELLOUS TO OTHERS.

A childhood friend, writes:

> *Dear Janice,*
> *I do want to say something about those awful memories of sexual abuse, and I hope you won't take this amiss, or as if it comes from someone who is excusing your father for what he did—but it seems to me, remembering Victor, that sexuality exuded from every pore, and he would no more be able to touch another human being without that being feeling a sexual response than Dixie! I mean, your dad handled the world as if it were flesh, you could see the way he ate, or played the piano, or danced, he was sexuality incarnate. Is it possible he didn't actually do anything purposeful but that as a child you felt this current and were repelled?*

THE LONGER I LOOK
AT THE PHOTOGRAPH,

or listen to the jazz riffs of Errol Garner's blind-bodied hands. The longer I look out across the green of this meadow's weeping willow. The longer I look … the longer I look at the photograph of my father, the more I am propelled backwards in time two decades to his death by drowning at 48, a suicide only those who loved him could decipher. The longer I look at the photograph of my father, the more audible his words: *I'm in such pain. I could take that rifle down from the wall and blow my brains out.*

The longer I look at the photograph. My father.

FATHER, IT MUST BE STATED RIGHT OFF,

was not always a good man, some would say. After a few rye and cokes, he sang Brazilian love songs at the piano about flying to the moon and adoration or spring. Sometimes his partying could "get out of hand."

> *And now it's the mouth*
> *The mouth and the tongue*
> *Pressed down*
> *To the faint smell of sea*

My father's death complicates my "new knowledge" of his molestation of me as a child. The complication begins precisely here in my brain, that most tender of erogenous zones. The space of desire for father, for his attentions. My longing for my father began I don't remember when. He sang songs at the piano that waited for love or the sun to fall from the sky.

At 16, I sobbed across the kitchen table, *please Father, I love you*. And he cried, *I love you*—the first time I remember him confessing this to me.

SHE DISCOVERS THE CATASTROPHE OF RESEMBLANCE:

the anxiety provoked through the encounter with something that paradoxically is experienced as at once foreign and familiar, distant and close, totally estranged, unknown, and at the same time strangely recognizable and known.

This afternoon, we make love. My lover is intense and passionate and I am remote, inside—not glacial but alluvial. Shifting, flat, not quite substantial. My father is the image on the wallpaper. He is my perimeter and peripheral vision. I am not safe. My fingernails bite hard into memory, the palm of my hand.

AS A SMALL CHILD, I RAN FROM
MY FATHER.

Making strange, my mother said.

Looking at the photographs, M says, *"You look just like him. Same colouring. Same cleft chin. Same pleasure in performance. Same temper—wild at times …"*

Her desire for him is a longing for someone at once foreign and familiar. Her organs secrete like any other, her body is recognizable as her own, her liver and her heart, of course. And the labial-laced pudenda, a familiar bone of contention rubbing here across my own. A breast or two inside the rhythm of two breaths exhaling syncopation. The gasp of recognition of you, and then I relax into a simple mantra … *likelikelikelikelike* … that leaves a trace in this sensation of suffocation.

The reflection of my father in the mirror at once *foreign and familiar* hovers above my arms wiring me to this circle of silvered glass. A fish weight anchors into heart ache; an ocean floor runs beneath us. Desire weaned into the proximity of this recognition. This *foreign and familiar body* crawling in next to you. Distant and close, as in to become totally estranged. (The too close recognition of the dark-haired body of sibling or parent.) Are we the catastrophe of incest?

HIS OWN GLOOM IS REFLECTED IN MINE.

I am no original, he said. *Your despair has become mine; mine, yours.*

Throw caution to the wind. Imagine your worst nightmare fleshed out at noon. You awaken, having not been asleep, and find your midnight self at play. Your movements look strange, perhaps merely "original." You discover you enjoy yourself, though "enjoyment" may not be an appropriate term. You anticipate companionable fears, welcome sleepless nights; weep for no apparent reason.

A mechanical watery beast ascends into your mouth. Aching with a desire not to open, your unhinged jaw tells you how to measure your words in silence. As you write, your nails rip open. The sting of fingers on fire, smoldering in the ache of your *mother*—I mean, *mouth*

You perform flawlessly.

Despair becomes your calling.

to depress *to lower in dignity, make undignified; to debase.*

Out of daily rhythms. The teacher tries to mark, to adjudicate others. Undone in the pain of judgment, she asks, *Who am I to judge in this failed mental state touched by petty stupidity, high anxiety, lost grip?* Procrastination with its paralysis, self-loathing and shame, so close to what she felt as a child. In the midst of this memory work, I lose my grip. Forget the exigencies of everyday life. What do I know in this state? The garden in drought. Dog longing for his leash.

In the interview, the critic tells her two things are operative in her writing—a critical sense and a psychological sense. *Your critical sense has been overwhelmed*, he says.

> depression as in *to bring into low spirits, to lower in station, fortune, or influence; to put down, to bring down, to humble.*

Here the line disappears between the one who makes the gun shake and the one who shivers in her boots, unbelieving. Scratch on the muzzle and the body winces. Not that *she* deserves it. Not that she is necessarily *she*. Not that he recalls himself to himself at the very moment his finger flicks open, her body below the horizontal.

Remember the Sticky Popeye, my brother reminds me. *I remember you telling me about the demon spinach-eater who chased you as a little girl.* I remember Sticky Popeye, the large punching bag that stood in the corner awaiting night to begin his slide across the floor to my bed, my body melting at the moment in an uncanny sensation of unspeakable childhood fear.

My brother and I compare our depressions. *You come by yours honestly,* I say, recalling the depressive history of each and every family member. *We're lucky there's been only one suicide,* he replies.

> depression as in this place: *This house depresses and chills one (1838).*

In this house, hands once stole underneath the covers as though invited there. The dead area I make my home. Windows board up with winter before it arrives. Shuttering.

How the wind soars through white pine, splintering all-season wolf-willow. Cut off. Cut down. Something forgotten surrenders, gets in the way. Between the eyes, memory's hairline root of focus contracts to looped circuits.

The way to leave sadness is not necessarily by the road to success. Try a lover, a beloved pet, a house…. (She wrote "a house" first, then erased it, not wanting to be perceived a vulgar materialist. But this was not the motive to finding herself in this house alone. In this house alone she found herself without the voices of parents who loathed each other. In this house alone, no one's hands stole under the covers unless she invited them there.)

depression   as in *to stammer.*

Words rip out of her mouth before spoken. Not exactly interruption. More like language shoved to the wrong side of the brain to play the *ratatatat* of magpies. Mimic this sound and try big words talking. *Depression* as in *to lower in pitch, to flatten (the voice or the musical note).* A hidden prairie song just like old tales told; their shopping list of melancholic lyrics almost obliterated in the white glow of freshly laundered sheets. Paper flaps like approximate wings.

I am not without compassion for what ailed you—your demons so carefully knotted at your throat each morning before you left for work. At night you let them out to play in the willows where I climbed, along the edge of the pond where I walked. Finger tips along the borders of my sheets, fold my desire into yours. Sometimes you sit right on the sill of the window I crept through to escape.

depression   as in *to put down by force, or crush in a contest or struggle; to overcome, subjugate, vanquish.*

What stood between her and her father's suicide. Her writing?

If I throw myself down this mountain, bruise the memory floating in this brain, carve up my arm (the vertical slash works best), breathe the hot fumes of automobile or oven, I will no longer be able to form these words with my fingers.

He sang: *I long to give you the moon trapped in the night of the sea.*

THIS SUICIDE MAKES HIS STORY
IMPOSSIBLE TO TELL.

This book was impossible to write.
This is not a book.
I have nothing to present.
This book is difficult.
To be present.
I have nothing.
A few pictures.
Scraps from the table.
Impossible to write.
This is not quite what I had in mind.

WHEN FATHER TOLD ME HE WAS GOING TO TAKE HIS RIFLE

from the wall rack and blow his head off, I told him he needed to see someone and to take up jogging, reduce his stress. *Getting your body in shape makes the world vanish,* I said as though knowing what would or could disappear. In response, he reached out his hand to show how skin peeled away from the flesh—the "prime" of life and his body already in decay.

Almost no one believed him.

Was that when he began to plot his drowning?

When I tell you this, you kiss me on the lips and give me an imperative "grow up" kind of talking to: *Stop being so melodramatic,* you say.

It doesn't help.

The problem is deeper.

Deep as the great blue sea.

THE SHHHHH SOUND OF OCEAN

sends her into sympathetic magic where being dissolves into his pain, now hers. What had justified this disaster? His long-suffering wife will not take him back for another round. Disenchanted, his new companion refuses to tolerate his bouts of drinking. For the moment, his distribution business fails and his dealings are under investigation. He surveys the snowmobiles lined up in warehouse drifts.

His suicide washes over her—the world fills up with water. No one lives outside the water, the flowing paralysis of time—nothing but this present without children, inheritance, or hope. Words too big for speech bubble through the glassy sea. His blue-roofed world swims below.

> *(Hush, don't speak, the sea doesn't like it when you don't pay attention to her. Swim. Stretch your arms up and churn the water, regularly, slowly, without restraint. Do you feel that you are turning into a dolphin? Do you feel the water's long caress dissolve your body ...)*

HE TOLD HER, "IT WAS AN ACCIDENT."

She couldn't help believing him. The first time. Suddenly. Out of the blue. Not a moment too soon. He was upon her. Accidentally. That's why she could barely remember the look in his eyes.

He invites her to feel how the skin peels from the backs of his hands. *"Nerves,"* he underscores with emphasis.

Incidentally, that's why she couldn't remember. *It was an accident.*

THE DEAD FATHER IS BURIED AGAIN.

This time his history shovels earth on his coffin. (Remember the day of his burial, the winter storm made the Brandon streets in January almost unpassable. As the coffin descends into the grave, my cousin peers over the edge. Unwittingly daring fate, his boots slide into the icy pit. With an ominous thud, the absurdity of his disappearance makes the mourners laugh. *"You can't take us with you."*

And yet you do. You dominate my dream last night again— this time as voiceover slipping on top of the main feature. My dream body stands in a fast flowing river, the rush of water hypnotic and frightening, especially when I lean against the wrought iron rail and it comes away in my hand. Fear again, and then from off screen, the sound of my front door opening, bells chiming with a voice that haunts familiar. My dreaming panic freezes at his greeting, *"Hello Jan...."*

Caught inside the grain of his voice, I am bored to death by my anxiety, my difficulty writing, reading, communicating, boredom a convenient substitute for fear.

Tonight I dream I am at sea, standing by my mother in the tropical blue, watching as my boy cousins and brothers cry out as they bend over to pull up starfish and stingrays, sea urchins and weeds. Paralyzed, with needle-sharp pricks in my soles, I can't look down. Suspended in a dead man's float, I await the touch of his hands.

Will I move towards the shore?

Q: HOW DOES THE STORY GO?

A: In abandoning me by drowning, he leaves me distraught, I dream up stories, imagine he is only too present, ever present, a sexually invasive man. This nightmare is partial compensation for his death. He wanted me too much.

I recreate news of his death. The telephone receiver cannot muffle the shock. I anticipate this moment of dread. How could I go out zombielike to shop with my lover that evening according to plan, acting "normal," as though furniture's lacquered presence could hold me together?

I tell the antique dealer that I can't decide about his mahogany chiffonier because my father washed up dead on a tropical beach that morning.

Oh, the man says, startled.

Yes, I continue, *drowned himself in the sea. Tied ropes to his waist. Anchored himself to a coral head. Suicide,* I say, eyes dead with grief.

I make a black skirt for the funeral—sewn up into a bag by mistake. Black worsted like the wool I imagine shrouds his limbs. The drowned body is flown north away from the sea.

IN 1975, HIS BODY BECOMES A QUESTION

that sounds through the years like his drowning.

Sometimes when I think about my father's suicide, in place of guilt or grief, I find a simple astonishing resentment. I resent his drowning. His last breath marked more than one death. I want him to come back to life so I can shake him into making sense of our loss. For a while I displace my rage anywhere. I resent the time it took for his friend to find his body on the lonely shore. His friend's tears of regret are real but why? Why hadn't he accompanied my father to the beach to swim?

After the funeral, my mother's voice sharpens. The shadow of my father passes through her words. Often expressionless, her eyes shift to empty. Occasionally horror, rage, regret, and sometimes fondness steal across her face. At night her lips mouth his name in dream.

IN 1975, HIS BODY BECOMES A WEAPON.

I wait in the anteroom of the funeral parlour, too fearful to view the corpse. His body brings him too close for comfort: reminding me of flesh and blood, powdered white to cover over the intensity of tan and watery bloat. His bones could be no more than disastrous debris the sea's lips spit up; skinned belly big with shells and scavengers.

My father's lover fantasizes how she could have saved him. This drives her mad with guilt and shame. She remembers how angry she had been the night before he flew south. How she refused to accompany him on this Caribbean vacation because of his pre-flight drinking binge. Undeserving of blame, B is haunted by a suicide's malignant ghost. When I go to meet her, she at first appears lifeless, barely sensing the disaster.

News of his death haunted her ear; his loss anchoring her in a long winter of excruciating madness. In the chapel, B's voice rises to a pitch I cannot replicate, *He's dead. What have they done to you? Oh Vic, what have they done?* She weeps her rage and my whole body shudders within her anguish. My own loss seems small in comparison—he was my father but we had not known each other, my childhood marked by our mutual retreat.

The sound of her desolation echoes through mundane rooms, unfit for the grandeur of inconsolable grief. Unprepared for this revelation of mourning and her collapse into the arms of her aunt and sister, I abandon her. Filled with her shattering cries, I don't remember returning home. In the weeks that follow, I don't remember visiting her though I know I do.

Tragedy proliferates, breeding on loss and suffering. After his death, her adolescent son disappears and she will never hear from him again. Suicide can murder those left behind.

TRYING TO MAKE SENSE OF HOW SUICIDE KILLS THE LIVING, I WRITE.

For those whose fathers considered suicide only to drown
There is no consolation

For those whose fathers considered suicide
A husband in his image waits in the wings

For those whose fathers commit suicide—the memory
Terror of the beach
Alone the knowledge of expansive sea turquoise to touch
The thigh the chest the breath the work
To be done to the death

For those whose fathers commit suicide
The fear for others the brothers
Perhaps the mother

For those whose fathers commit suicide
The urge to confess
Your hatred at his flight

For those whose fathers commit suicide
The outrage
Being outdone undone stood up till your dying day

For those whose fathers considered suicide
no kamikaze culture
enfolds your horror.

For those whose fathers commit suicide
An open book
an unfinished reading.

B WAS NOT ONLY ONE OF MY FATHER'S MANY AFFAIRS,

but the woman my father chose to live with after separating from my mother. In a photograph taken on Roatin Island where my father had established something of a colonial holiday site, B, delicate, beautiful and at ease, masquerades as one of Gauguin's maidens. Long black braids and colourful sarong exoticize my father simply by her proximity to his midlife paunch. His pearly smile sets his deeply tanned skin in relief.

As a child, my fights with my father often focused on our skin colour. At dinner he would tell me how lucky I was to be born white with a good-sized brain and none of the imaginary genetic contaminants of a less 'pure' genealogy. Eager to establish my distance from him, I resisted this line of reasoning early enough in my teen years that when he denounced me as *artsy crafty lefty*, my feigned resentment hid bafflement at the meaning of his intended insult. My father's racism became an aspect of his person that I could study and understand. I knew that racism was learned and unjust so when I was invited to the United Nations with other student winners of a public speaking contest, I searched out a book on racism for my father. He didn't read it then, but how would he react to recent family disclosures that my maternal great great grandmother was a southern Ontario Mohawk?

RACISM WORKS TO TIE UP THE LOOSE
ENDS FEAR UNRAVELS.

How did my father reconcile his love for B, an Asian
Canadian woman, with his earlier racism? B's own refusal to
continue to collaborate in his alcoholic fantasy and accompany him on his final travels south was a courageous decision
on her part that could have provided him with an opening
for a different possible future—had he chosen to live.

I reread my poem:

> *For those whose fathers considered suicide*
> *no kamikaze culture*
> *enfolds your horror.*

B figures in these lines as though her memory leaks into my
poem. In retrospect, I know these *kamikaze* lines ring hollow.
Did my father's racist diatribes during my childhood enable
my too easy use of the "kamikaze" to signal cultural difference?

As I sit alone in a darkened theatre, B's cries haunt me still. I
weep for the movie's young Japanese widow who contemplates taking her own life years after her young husband's suicide. Her memories are mad with death. When her new
husband finds her wandering the seashore drawn to a burning
funeral pyre, he tries to console her, *The sea has a tendency to
beguile.... It happens to all of us.*

"MY TRUTH ISN'T YOURS,"

my brother Ward says when he tells me about our father:

> My father was a man looking for something really beautiful. He pushed and lived right on the edge. What is profound is how far he fell—he was in pure terror the last six months of his life. His breakdown was so catastrophic, his secretary Mary told me he sometimes fell out of his chair at work.
>
> Without the education or insight to comprehend what it was he was looking for, he didn't understand you could strive after higher things and still be human. He was looking for a kind of transport and he had that dynasty thing you know, bound for greatness. Even buying that property in the Caribbean—those stupid aristocratic ideas about our family. The island of Roatin was where he could be king for a day—to be king and then throw away the crown for everybody. To make, then break class barriers. Just before he died he was fascinated by the Nixon trial and how ambition could be so destructive.
>
> Dad was so gifted. A minor version of King Lear—so tragic ... he couldn't find anyplace called home.
>
> And his death was so amazing—the thought that went into his decision to protect us from the knowledge of his death. Going back to the islands for a holiday. Saying goodbye to us all even though we didn't recognize his farewell. Even giving Mom power of attorney and pretending it was necessary for some urgent business deal. He wanted to disappear mysteriously and leave us with the life insurance.
>
> Mom said she thought he died of three things: a bad marriage, ambition, and alcoholism. But imagine staging your own death. To drown in that turquoise water all alone one brilliant tropical day. That's high tragedy.

IN DREAM, FATHER RETURNS TO ME DIFFERENTLY.

Costumed in an old man's white beard, I hardly recognize him in his robes, tattered by wind-swept moors. Frigid air escapes from the flowing folds as he describes his last act: he performs death impeccably. Just like the father who stands at the edge of the subway platform thinking about the future. Without a revealing word or tremor, his head leans forward as though checking the wind. His face pivots away from the approach of the train as the driver's eyes widen into the terror that will shatter any family. He knows what is inevitable: his death, their lifelong mourning. But his deadly performance guarantees one small gift—the insurance money.

And the nothing he passes on.

From: Ward Williamson
Sent: March 24, 1998 7:22 PM
To: Janice Williamson
Subject: Brilliant

Janice—I was just thinking what a fantastic conception your idea of using Dad's life/death as a meditation on your own feminist concerns. You get right at the heart of the matter by dealing with the relationship with your father. That's one thing amazing. But, the story of his death is out of some opera and raises it to another level altogether. You have something really rare in terms of material to work with. I can never tell if I am being harsh when I speak my mind, but if I was last night, it is only to stress the importance of getting it right. This is almost a myth; and when something like this knocks at your door it seems to me it's from an authentic muse and to let her down is a sort of blasphemy. So extend yourself. In order to deal with father to some extent you have to descend into his hell. It is a very serious place to fall into. If you want a clue to the mythical dimensions of it, stuff like Hercules' death—the poison shirt Nessus gave him—unendurable pain the more he wrestled with it the worse it got. You can think that his major consideration was providing for his family, but I am of the opinion that the last judgement being passed on Dad caused him to totally reevaluate his life. That is why his death is to me more in the order of an atonement. I don't think you understand him unless you realize he had a high sense of honour. And honour is something—and I think most men are unconscious of this fact—that is very important to anyone of any integrity (read *Lord Jim*—the best book on honour ever written). I think his father, as Mom I'm sure will tell you, was responsible for instilling in him a sense of goodness, of honour. He had betrayed these principles through drinking, through shady business dealings, and through a stupid and selfish disregard for others. I think his death was an act of a man trying to redeem himself. And I don't think he could have lived. This is a very complex issue and touches again on the tragedy of his environment. What he was searching for was not even recognized, in fact is hated, in the environment he existed in. If he had lived he would have been a shadow of what he wanted to be. I think this is what most, if not all, the terror was about.

At any rate the story has some interesting dimensions; which is in reality I guess, in counterpoint to your own meditation on women and oppression etc. and your own feelings towards Dad. If I were you I would spend at least another year writing it. Don't rush it.

sorry for getting so involved.

PS—I wonder if honour is an authentic thing in a man. It certainly is important to me. Something about independence but also something sublime, beautiful.

TO "ACCOMPANY" HER

> *Who is this patient when she posits the event as real, who is she when she deems it unreal? We need to "accompany" her among her family members, identifying, for example, the person who wants to disguise a shameful event (like a suicide, madness, incest, violent crimes, an illegitimate birth). In another case, someone is trying to confuse a child by saying, What you thought you saw was only a dream. This patient's hesitations between reality and fantasy aim at recreating, in the analyst, the sense of bewilderment he himself experienced as a child.*

I want to *accompany* myself among my family members. Look for signs and signals. Alert myself to the way we revisit, turn away from and return to our past. At night I dream I take my brothers' hands as we take our time finding our childhood driveway. Small boys at my side, big sister in the middle takes the lead, though sometimes I follow in their footsteps. In the raised stone garden beside the gate, outlandish purple iris bloom. Willow trees stalk the hillside. A dog barks. Curtains rustle remembering the touch of unseen hands. We are home and once again there is fear and love and a large lick of memory in our hearts.

All of us have suffered. Each has risked madness. We work as artists, writing, sculpting, painting, making our way through to a life. Sometimes out of touch with each other, we couldn't risk intimacy, fearful that this too might be accompanied by catastrophe. Withholding, we waited for a response when silence had already spoken.

The border is a swing door. Now in touch, we warm to each other.

WHAT WOULD FATHER SAY IF HE COULD LISTEN?

Yes, says the man when the girl now woman visits to tell him how he touched her here and here and put his cock there and there and how he made her feel so bad and then yummy inside until she didn't want to sometimes she didn't. And then she did anyway because he said she would or she was bad or he would be mad and then when they found out she would feel like this or that but not in any way good or happy like little girls should.

The dirty old man.

**TO READ WITHOUT WRITING
IS TO SLEEP.**

Despair travels through time: the father, a suicide; the mother, a depressive; the brothers, are whipped into the expressive centre of the arts by their own bleak demons. The eldest sister winters here at the keyboard, eyes ringed insomniac.

Midnight, and melodrama on the lips of women's novels gives some relief. Mary Shelley's heroine laments

But my father, my beloved and most wretched father? Would he die? Would he never overcome the fierce passion that now held pitiless dominion over him? Might he not many, many years hence, when age had quenched the burning sensation that he now experienced, might he not then be again a father to me?

Mathilda's story sounds too familiar; the parallels, uncanny: father/daughter incest, horror, confession, suicide, and incurable melancholy. *She transmits a tale to a reader, but almost posthumously, as if to extinguish the possibility that its reading will change anything, for her or in the world.* And indeed, the manuscript did not change anything. She sent it to her father, publisher and author William Godwin, who refused to return the manuscript condemning the topic as *disgusting and detestable,* and advising that *there ought to be, at least if it is ever published, a preface to prepare the minds of the readers for the fall of the heroine.* Lost in her father's papers, the manuscript wasn't published until 1959, 150 years after its writing.

I WANT TO CHANGE THE WORLD.

IN 1996, MY BODY BECOMES A QUESTION

(D. says, *It's about time. When you approach 48, you'll revisit your father's death. Ask him to teach you what he didn't know himself.*)

This book lives inside me long enough for words to become dangerous parasites. I recall my father's death by practicing my own. My body fails, organs explode and are disappeared.... *We then extended our incision slightly toward the left of the umbilicus ... into frank, purulent, pus cavity....*

I maintain myself in a constant state of emergency. Ambulance sirens ring through the neighbourhood so often people stop me on the street to remark about the urgency of my demise. Lungs fill up with a cry, collapse in fear. Reproductive organs swell and atrophy. The fibre-eating anachronism, my appendix, bursts and spells uncertain doom....

Stones rip through the bile-filled sack until I am flayed thin. Shit. The mess of it running down my legs; my feet mired in the drudgery of corporeal dread. Fingers of hurried nurses tease out the tubes' translucent lines from belly, nose, and wrist.

Morphine fulfills pleasure's carelessness, cuts through monstrous dreams of death.

I REMEMBER HIS LIPS,

fleshy and fulsome like mine, my youngest brother's, my nephew's. Full of fear or anger, love-making or crooning to some musical riff only imagined by others.

My mother dreams my dead father returns to weep inconsolably about something mysterious. Out of the blue, she calls me to say she has cancelled her vacation and plans to visit the following week. She doesn't tell me about her dream and how the mystery unravels as other mourners enter the dream room grieving my death at 45. When my mother arrives, a friend greets her at the airport and then drives her to the emergency ward where I have rushed earlier that afternoon with mysterious undiagnosable pains. My illness lingers on for weeks in the hospital where I undergo a battery of tests. *Cancer? No! Heart attack? No! Intestines? No! Lungs? No! Womb? No!*

I am 45 and too young to die, I announce dramatically. My mother sits by my side day after day never explaining her premonition of my illness, her fear of my imminent death. We talk about my father and explain how much we both loved him, appreciated so much of what he was. His wit. Wild energy. Musical joy. Love of parties and celebrations, friends and beautiful places. We talk in the knowledge of his failings, losses, pain—and our invisible wounds. We do not speak of forgiveness or guilt or sin, unimportant words in our familial vocabulary and spiritual need. We speak as though our world of rage and anger had exploded to make space for wave upon wave of memory. Entire newsreels of sensate story unroll before us in the dreary hospital room. His dark skin in summer glows against the imagined green-wet lawn. His lips, his shining teeth disappear in a whirl of snow. My mother and I remember this February afternoon.

Ektomy: A Chance Betrayal

Whenever we turn in the storm of roses, thorns illuminate the way.

INGEBORD BACHMANN

I will make what does not exist, exist. I will do it and appease my greed to acquire more of life, more of what vanishes, more of my own (im)mortality; will remember what I cannot remember with Kodak pictures.... I have more life in me (we) than you think.

MARY MELFI

ROOTING IN THE DICTIONARY,

she finds her entrance to writing her body's suffering in the word:

> ektomy *to cut out*
> *Gr. epsilon-kappa-tau-omicron-mu—eta—excision*
> *(f. epsilon-kappa—out + tau-epsilon-mu-nu-epsilon-iota-*
> *nu—to cut)*

Cut doesn't find its contemporary meaning until the sixteenth century. Earlier, the word stood alone in the phrase *to draw cuts* indicating the drawing of lots or "cuts," sticks or straws of unequal lengths in games of chance.

   Ektomy, she thinks, *a chance betrayal.*

[CUT]

**THE PATHETIC BODY REMAINS
TOO CLOSE FOR COMFORT.**

She does not want to expropriate her body's suffering but to distill its meaning and understand. Were she to read her crimped agonizing breaths through the I word, she could sound victim rather than subject of suffering. She cannot anticipate the readings: the cynical, the generous, the patronizing, the appropriative, the empathic.

Cautious: she wants to tell a story with the I word and won't.

[CUT]

HER SICK BODY IS HER FASHION BODY.

After a few months she still fits easily into the teenage pack rat clothes of thirty years ago. Bones replace flesh. The world announces itself in the edges of things.

[CUT]

EDMONTON, ALBERTA, JULY 1996:

She wants to theorize her body but remembers how the
Greek *theor* is one who travels to see things. She has very little distance to travel. Can she be a tourist at what might be
her own funeral? She wishes she had her camera and tripod
to take a self-portrait, but her morphine and opium-driven
fascination with the present moment fathoms no more than
"today is afternoon" as she watches the play of shadow across
the sun-blazed hospital wall. Kyoko, a friend, enters the hospital room, takes one look at the body in the bed, *her* body,
and bursts into tears. At first, the suffering body does not recognize tears as a sign of horror. Then she sees how her body
has been made strange to her.

As a child, a recurring nightmare accompanied any serious
fever. She imagined her body melting in her bed, her flesh an
oozing mess across the floor. Frightened at the memory, she
leaps out of her skin, and unbound, hears a strange sucking
wheezing sound as an arcane machine drains stomach bile.
Eyes open now to the terror in Kyoko's face, she traces the
tubes' sinuous paths from stomach through nose, from ure-
thra to sack. Look. The thin rubber hose is clamped to the
incision. The twisted feeding line enters wrists and fingers,
now blackened, now blue.

[CUT]

FALLIBLE . . . FALLING . . . FALLOW . . .

In bed tonight, she squints at the fine print:

> fallible *liable to be erroneous, unreliable;* ... Falling-star ... Fallopian—*Latinized name of an Italian anatomist (1523-1562) Used in the names of certain anatomical structures reputed to have been discovered by Fallopius.*

She lost her womb twice: once when almost too young to notice and again in a summer not long ago. The first time she lost her womb, ruby sails drain February light.

Tonight her womb is missing. *Womb*, she says, *goodbye.*

[CUT]

PITTSBURGH, PENNSYLVANIA,
JUNE 1975

Six months almost to the day after the suicide of her father, she marries in the family garden. Guests cry at the wedding, not at the sentimentality of the occasion, but in memory of the absent guest, her father. She cries too, in secret, in her parent's bedroom where the wedding gown swept across the bed, her body crushed by the weight of its promise. She had married a man just like her father—a bargain with a past to ensure future suffering. A wedding guest stumbles by accident into the room. His apology cannot mask the sorrow of his knowing glance.

Six months later the bride's body bursts open on a moonless night. Fallopian tubes swell beside twisted ovaries, abscessed and throbbing with fire. Thus begins a long story of IUD's and infection, misdiagnoses and masked symptoms, fainting and falling. Explaining in a language she could not understand, surgeons grew eager to empty her body, promising to cut out the offensive organs through microscopic scars.

Her new husband collapses with the news of her barrenness; his love dissipates in the knowledge his wife will not carry his offspring to birth. He abandons her in stages. First, he never looks into her eyes or caresses her. At breakfast, he eats in silence, leaving early in the day to return home late at night. Over the next few months she too finds herself holding back feelings, veiling desire. As she grows mute, hollow and inert, furniture in the abandoned rooms become companions.

One night, she imagines life returned to the time before. In the bath, she splashes him with water, a playful gesture not quite masking her resentment. The edge of something is breached and unburdened. All she recalls of that moment he thrusts her head under the water's surface is how the blueness of his eyes condenses to translucent vapour. Or was it ice?

His hands, now powerful weapons, hold her body underwater. Bruised and urgent, she kicks and kicks: her left foot, then the right smashes into faucet and handles. As her head pushes to the surface for frantic breath, he catches her frightened look. What was the thought that interrupted his actions? Startled for a moment, he finds himself in the act of drowning his wife. It had been a little more than a year since her father had drowned himself and they had wed. How could he explain his wife's fate worse than death—a watery repetition, uncanny in its echoes?

[CUT]

A DIFFERENT UNEXPECTED
DRAMA UNFOLDS:

fueled by dreams of lineage and genes, my husband is unable to come to terms with my infertility. One night, inexplicably, he tries to drown me in the bath. When this tactic fails (sudden remorse? loss of will? slippery grip?), he terrorizes me in the night, throwing the main electrical switch. Pitched into darkness, I crawl naked down the stairs, envisioning a flight across the lawn to the safety of the neighbours beyond. As my eyes dart about the room in frightened anticipation, my husband awaits at the bottom of the stairs, meets my stare with his new mad eyes, fierce with blue anger. For a moment, I hesitate on the step, remember my own longing for a child, my hopelessness and fear. Recalling that supplication can save, I creep towards him on my knees, accompanied by the knowledge that feigned blind submission may tame his rage. Apologies shower across his body. Grasping at legs wet with my tears, I entreat him to love me again, in spite of my barrenness. After three days, I run away from home for good.

[CUT]

SIX YEARS AFTER SHE LEAVES HIM, THEY MEET AGAIN

in the home of a well-meaning mutual friend who invites both of them, uninformed of the other's presence, for dinner. Her ex-husband arrives with his new wife, a thin dark-haired woman, intense and nervous at his side, along with their two children, a little girl, and an infant son.

I would like you to meet my wife, Janice, Janice, he says, blue eyes sparkling with delight at the repetition. This echo would have been comical to the women too, were it not the case that he passed the evening telling the second wife Janice that when he looked at his children, he thought of them as his first wife, Janice's. The second wife Janice cried in the kitchen for the duration of the dinner. The first wife Janice preferred oblivion to conversation: consuming vast quantities of wine, this first wife (a drunken me) cunningly passed out beside the children on the living room floor.

She doesn't remember their departure and has not seen them for 20 years. Perhaps they live somewhere in North America. Perhaps Europe. Today the little girl Clare will be 20. Perhaps Clare turns this page, enraged at the knowledge of her father's history. Perhaps she disbelieves the woman who might have been a mother had her body not betrayed her.

[CUT]

IN THE UNDERWORLD, SHE SEES
THE DEVIL,

makes love to the jester and eats her fill of seeds and berries, begging for a child to dull the pain of her own mortality. She is rendered infertile; her womb will not bear offspring, ever. Nor will children spring forth like Zeus's head-trip Aphrodite.

When the stars fall from out of the sky, Demeter discovers her daughter Persephone has been kidnapped. Grieving her filial loss, the entire world is pitched into black unending mourning. Baubo, an old woman, lifts up her skirts to reveal her naked body, sagging lips vital with desire and love of life. The pleasure in Demeter's surprised look teaches her something. Uncertain about what it is she sees, she knows it has to do with what is suspended between them: the knowledge of her daughter and something other than her daughter. Something they share, and something they don't.

The sight of Baubo's pudenda inspires Demeter to uproarious laughter. What does she see but pleasure in the here and now? Tears run down her cheeks to fill parched river valleys with rushing streams.

In spring, Persephone will return from the land of the dead to her mother who tends at her bedside wishing her to life again.

[CUT]

THE DAUGHTER REMEMBERS
HER OWN PANIC.

I remember my own panic. I am in the hospital. Age 24. Married six months, I collapse on Boxing Day, suffer excruciating pain. A sudden diagnosis of something: cancer, cysts, PID. (This catalogue of ailments is a relief after months of accusations: *It's all in your head....*) A doctor claims he will fix me even though he doesn't know what is wrong. A sick lamb, I am shepherded from here to there. My body is tackled as *problem* and threatened with a hysterectomy that will turn me inside out, bring the "problem" to light. I refuse to sign the surgery consent form, *I'm too young and don't trust you.* Nonetheless, nurses are requested to shave my pubic hair, give me an enema. The next morning, supported with the advice of another doctor, I check myself out of the hospital. *Scared.*

Childless. Scarred for life, but it doesn't feel like a scar. More like fate or leaving home, an exit from the suburbs and housewifely duties. A way out of my mother's sadness, her screaming sleepless nights. What were my chances of winding up hating or cursing or wishing him dead?

ON TURNING 40, I VISIT
THE GYNECOLOGIST.

For the first time, I cry when she inserts the speculum. *Don't worry*, I try to explain, *recent memories of incest make my body feel painfully vulnerable.*

A moment later, I realize my explanation is a mistake and only grants permission for the gynecologist to mutate into pop psychologist fortune teller. Grounding her hypotheses in my history, she tells me my fear of my father is displaced rage about the gynecologist who once tried to coerce the 24-year-old me into a hysterectomy.

Oh yeah, I drawl snidely, *and you're Sigmund Freud.*

TWENTY YEARS AFTER HER DIVORCE, SHE MAKES PLANS TO ADOPT

an orphaned girl from China, so far away. There are meetings with other adoptive parents surrounded by shy or energetic little girls, jet-haired and animated. Long-distance telephone calls with women who have travelled all the way to Beijing to meet their ward dressed in frilly clothes for the first time. As she begins the paperwork, her body collapses into a mess of infection and twisted organs. Hospitals transformed into bureaucratic ineffectiveness shift her between wards, diagnoses, and doctors. Nothing remains between her and the fiction that becomes her body but blank agony.

Dreaming about her daughter's death, her mother tells her she wants to be the first to die. Nonetheless, the daughter finds herself silently rehearsing her last will and testament the night before surgery. The hydrocephalic gigantism of tubes and ovaries are excised through a thick hook-shaped incision along her belly. Throughout the autumn, she bleeds intermittently: her hair falls out; thin threads of brown turn grey.

[CUT]

SHE WILL NOT . . . SHE CAN NOT
BEAR CHILDREN.

She is rendered infertile—*not fertile; unfruitful, unproductive, barren, sterile.* Her first thought: *now I can write and have a different life than the one I planned*—as though her writing and child-not-to-be inevitably interweave.

At first infertility grants her a certain liberation from her fears of domestic relationships. In matters of love, her commitment to noncommitment becomes ever more adamant as she arms herself against any male lover's desire for a child. Female lovers are safer prospects. Adoption remains out of the question as she remains "too busy."

Over the years, the topic of infertility becomes urgent as other women of her generation approach their forties only to discover their barrenness as they try to reproduce. The woman friend who miscarries recounts in agony how the inside of her body falls onto the floor where she looks for signs as though the fetus could speak in the lost language of flesh and blood.

Is the air of neoconservative political retrenchment wherein the non-mothering woman as dangerous harbinger of unwanted change and crisis responsible for the pathos of the infertile woman? Or is it simply the frustrated desire on her part? This question does not contain the irretrievable loss.

[CUT]

SOMETIMES OUR STORIES
ARE UNSPEAKABLE

even to those who might share in suffering the loss, the rage. In the early 80s, a childhood friend calls to tell her she is in hospital undergoing treatment for her infertility caused by a similar episode of pelvic inflammatory disease. They talk and she promises to visit and continue their conversation. Never will she call to reengage and talk. They do not see each other again. Childlessness is a subject too painful to broach for more than a decade.

Hospitalized in the mid-90s, she finds herself in her friend's position: another woman refuses to acknowledge her illness. As though no longer her friend, she ignores the weeks in hospital and her suffering. She too has had her encounter with infertility. Fifteen years before, her first husband, now a father of two children by another woman, left for good as she recuperated from surgery in the hospital. Since then, her body has become the topic of her research. Over time she begins to think of her torso as a ship sailing through sharp coral-edged corridors, an ample empty vessel to support her thinking head.

[CUT]

DURING A VISIT TO NEW DELHI, HER CANADIAN FRIEND TELLS HER

she is not paying enough attention to her three-year-old child. The garden, dust-filled and barren, fills with afternoon smog, thick on the trail of a traffic jam like no other. August arrives and with it crystalline heat, days emptied but for the wandering snake charmer and the women who offer rags and children. The child is everywhere in her friend's daily life, the inside-out story of her days: motherhood a rationale for agoraphobia.

The visitor feels her limbs amputated by grief. Inside the house, the child plays with his box of toys. Oblivious, the woman reaches across the table for water, light, a pen; the cool breeze of memory plays across her face.

These two women, no longer friends, will not meet again. The trace of barrenness and motherhood mark each of them until their bodies no longer speak to each other. One fills her days with the particular rhythms of feeding and early talk, transformed into someone called *mother.* The other contents herself with surrogate nurturing. Her students visit with tales of accomplishment or great pain. Adopted children accompany her to plays or walks. One day she and a borrowed seven-year-old niece stop along the ravine to find the hole in a tree trunk where the fairies live. The little girl presses her ragged note into the soft loam inside the dark, securing it with a flat rock. The note lives in the tree trunk until rains wear the fibres into dreams. They do not return to find the fairy's gifts of licorice or the paints of many colours. She wonders: Were she a mother, would she be more responsive to bare wishes?

[CUT]

ON LOSING HIS BABY SON,

Mallarmé writes of an inexpressible love:

> *Mère, pleure*
> *Moi, je pense.*
> Mother, weep
> Me, I think.

And what of the mother who writes, the writer who thinks and mothers? Or the woman who weeps in the name of the child she never births? *I think Mother. I weep and write.* The death of my child is imaginary. Pregnancy never occurred. Birth escaped me in spite of hot pursuit. I am she with the will to mother—she who mourns her failed desire and watches the children at the playground. There is no consolation for the woman who witnesses despair at a distance.

[CUT]

THIS CITY SHELTERS AN ARMY OF CARRIAGES,

silver spokes spin from cafe to sandbox where evenings, paper cups disguise wine or scotch from the uninitiated. Mothers and fathers swing children. But afternoons nannies from the Philippines or the Caribbean gather in vibrant groups for conversation and laughter. Later, neighbourhood streets fade to dusk's sienna in their absence.

[CUT]

THE MANUSCRIPT SITS ON THE TABLE ALONGSIDE HIS BABY PICTURES.

Over the years, they meet for lunch, restaurants around the city fill with unspoken erotic conversations rippling across her skin. He overhears them too. His stories roam towards the pleasures and dangers of family. Hers, of work. Her manuscript sits as white as the tablecloth beside his empty plate. The typeface floats before him, arranged so he can read his own frustrated desire. Every year they meet, he talks about his children: the one who came before is always loved; the one on the way, a surprise, or his wife's desire. Until the birth. When the register of family portraits is displayed: the infant at breast feeding, sibling angled awkwardly into the frame, leaning into another new sister. He, the father, the invisible photographer.

She doesn't reciprocate offering snapshots of her monstrous poodle in the park, or her friends or students, the neighbours who wave to her each day. She talks about adoption and then, after her illness, of her body split open.

[CUT]

IN OCTOBER, FRUIT ROTS
IN THE FIELDS.

Each time her body fails her, she is about to have a child, the first time, by birth, the second by desire. Perhaps she should read the signs backwards: each time she is about to have a child, her body cracks open as though warning her of what is to be lost or gained. She imagines this vulnerability will be the death of her.

In the end, will she remain childless, explaining it is less dangerous this way?

[CUT]

GO TO THE CAFE AND PRETEND YOU ARE
IN A FOREIGN CITY WRITING.

Imagine that your favourite activity is wandering. Anything that looks like home repels you. Anticipation of the domestic accelerates your desire for flight. Imagine how you hold the pen between index and thumb, gripped just so to indicate a European flair, complemented by the double espresso (long) beside you on the table. You are in a cafe remembering the evening in Provençe you sat (alone) thinking about what it would be like to be thinking about this moment twenty years hence. The moment has arrived. In this recollection you find yourself thinking not about the wild boar bleeding before you or the small sounds of bird skeletons crackling between the teeth of the couple seated nearby or the taste of the wine from Luberon (too full) or the way your black lace dress cuts a fine figure, slight and melancholic to suit the times. You think about a woman in a cafe alone, thinking about the future, imagining how she will be surrounded by a child, a lover, a family. Or she thinks at that moment in the Provençal cafe that she will be alone at the table twenty years hence and that is all right too—solitude a relief from conflict or boredom or exhaustion or a combination therein that might have been were you not sitting here at the table. Alone and writing fragments that begin ... *whenever we turn in the storm of roses....*

[CUT]

ONE'S OWN TRAUMA IS TIED UP
WITH THE TRAUMA OF ANOTHER ...

> *Trauma may lead, therefore, to the encounter with another, through the very possibility and surprise of listening to another's wound.*

Near the end, this book began to write itself while I took time out for love. On our second meeting, in the middle of our lives, we hear echoes in parallel histories. The story G. tells is set in a northern city of childhood summers shattered by winter. As a two-year-old, he remembers his mother and then she is gone. Abandonment has no explanation. The children, all five of them, carry on with their father and aunts. Many years later G. arranges to meet his mother, is delighted in her glorious energy, their common traits. He finds another home in her and waits years for another meeting when he can tell her of his longing, for her, her love.

On our third tryst, G. and I drive to the edge of the city where a telescope magnifies Mars 180 times. Pulsing red and other-worldly, the planet appears to speed so quickly across the sky the astronomer must shift the lens every few moments in order to keep Mars in sight.

It's just the rotation of the earth, he explains as we look at our feet planted side by side.

Later in bed, G. and I caress and kiss on the lips so hard our pillows hollow out in feathered heaps. If we pushed any harder, we might fall through the centre of the earth all the way to China. Nothing can stop us now that we've listened to what it is that ails us and doesn't, how it is we came to be here on this earth-bound edge of spring, within sight of a red planet flashing this message that we read to you—this overdue recognition, a remedy called love.

[CUT]

ON SUNDAY MORNING HER LOVER IS SLEEPY, INWARD, SELF-CONTAINED.

She wants to make love or at least caress. He seems disinterested so she gets up and has a bath. Before his morning cigarette on the porch, he brings her coffee. He says he won't respond to her out of fear she always sexualizes intimacy. He will make her breakfast and listen to her say she feels like damaged goods, too sexually demanding and excessive, too reductive in her desire. She imagines he will abandon her, and he asks, *Why?* Later he will kiss her body all over and she will not confess she wants to make love and he says nothing and she wonders for a moment what he wants.

To find her way through this labyrinthine desire, she crosses the room and enters her study. Turning on her laptop, she writes about spoons and the pleasures of sugar in her bowl.

WHEN MAKING LOVE,
PEOPLE THE ROOM

with ghosts of your own choosing:

- one lusty feather-breasted trickster, with wings that furl up when aroused
- a peacock to take care of looking
- a dancing girl who talks a mile a minute, tutu drooping in the heat
- a storyteller to refuse fixed walls
- a muscle man who thinks
- a plumber to repair the works
- a big black poodle who dreams the proceedings in whimpers

Demand enough variety to suit your needs and some left over for surprises.

THIS MORNING YOUR HANDS FIT
LIKE A ROUGH MITT.

the curve of her stomach shows a T-bone trace of scalpel and kiss. When you describe how the navel looks just like the eye of the round in the butcher's map, she knows you are made for each other: carnivorous and hungry.

[CUT]

THIS IS NOT A HAPPY ENDING.

Romance is for always and ever only sublime romance.

Soon the swamp world of memory seeps in. Mothers parade across the pillow cases, outstretched arms threaten in their plenitude. Neglectful fathers will their way to freedom, gnawing at the inside of the frame until not even your smile remains.

Nonetheless, hilarity reigns when it could have been too late. Every Wednesday, two of us might tickle each other to death. Or a woman might sweep across the sheets to replace our romantic hero. It could be worse: we might have ignored the whole damn story.

[CUT]

. . . INTO A SMALL WORD . . .

Stones are old money with which we rent the work,
*   forgetting that the landscape borrows us*
For its own time and its own reason.

... i ... embedded *in* endings so familiar. The one who marries or the one who gets away. Walks into the ocean, calm now this afternoon. Or rips off her car to drive into the nowhere one morning. The ending so familiar, I can barely tear her away from the inevitable gasp, the cranky tinge of regret for the familiar. How I falls, stones in her pocket or her hands. Stones held close enough; I can read the signs. Stones with sea shells pocking their surface. I lingers here. Puts them in her pocket like Virginia and starts her descent. The grasses so thick at the edge of the pond, I stumbles towards the water. Her breath faster, a sobbing shore. Tracking towards the depths, I is reminded of her fall. Her failure. Her pocketed fingers play along the surface of ridged stones, rubbing them into warmth, as though alive again. Swirls of plant life etched on their surface could be feathers or birds. I lingers here, a landscape photographer who skirts the cliff to climb. The woods linger so thick near the bottom, I barely escape their rooms. Higher up, her breath comes in slow beats. The dog in her loose now. Fixing herself along the crest, her steps a reminder of her progress. Looking back, I finds another woman and perhaps a man, so small in the distance, they could be animals in this fighting wild.

Ascent means something other than up here. Five stones spread on this summit are chilled on the rocky outcrop. Five smooth stones fill her palm with satisfaction. I does not have to return again and again to replenish this standing here. Once is enough. Around her, I finds herself in a tent of stones. Silver pebbles tossed up in a fit of fabled care or rage litter the sky. Stone steps up and down the hillside mark a trail past cairns.

Imagine the voices which have carried them here. I wants to imagine this place beyond the violence of retribution and exploited sensation. Beyond abandonment too. Straining her eyes into the dark street below, I is certain they have left her alone. I calls and calls into the deserted alley until she hears them shout from above. When they meet for a good talk, this roof of quiet locates her, filled with welcoming laughter, just beyond your sight.

Adorable Dora
(What Dora Had In Mind When She Was Writing)

Dora had for some time suffered from various hysterical symptoms (nervous cough, loss of voice, migraine, depression, and what Freud calls "hysterical unsociability" and "taedium vitae"), but it was not until the autumn of 1900, when her parents found a suicide note from her, that Dora's father sent her to Freud for treatment.... She believes (and Freud agrees) that she is being used as a pawn in a game between her father and Herr K., the husband of her father's mistress. The father wants to exchange Dora for Frau K.... so as to be able to carry on his affair with Frau K. undisturbed. Dora claims that her father only sent her to psychiatric treatment because he hoped that she would be "cured" into giving up her opposition to her father's affair with Frau K., accept her role as a victim of the male power game, and take Herr K. as her lover....

Freud himself is the first to admit that his treatment of Dora is a failure.

Toril Moi

I am what Dora would have been if the history of women had begun.

Hélène Cixous

The problem of the referent was a source of constant struggle between Freud and Dora ... and finally, in an oblique way, halted the progress of the analysis, since Freud insisted on too

Rec'd
May 23/54

076X

*narrow a referential frame (by his own admission) for Dora's
symptoms. That is, he framed the case around the male prin-
cipals, completely excluding Dora's mother, and failing to
recognize Frau K. as a possible object of Dora's desire as well
as her identification.*

SHARON WILLIS

THE CASE OF THE MISSING KEY

[*from Dora's journal*] **August 10**

I love L! Herr K's wife, the woman I call "adorable," a pearl
of a love. That's why I call her "L."

Coughed all day in response to a frightful dream. Herr K.
came to my room last night. This is more than a dream. Of
this I am certain, though I can tell no one because I remember the event as though it were nothing more than a dream.

The key went missing. I began to lock myself in my room
after the walk in the garden when he drew me to him and
kissed me to my horror. My uncle, Father's best friend, kissing me in the garden. I told no one. I asked L for a key to
lock my room, pretending my bad dreams scared me. A lock
will make me feel safe.

Last night as usual I wanted to lock the door, but the key was
missing. Missing! I knew of course he had stolen it. I dreamt
he came into my room. In the morning I remember the
dream that he had come to my room. Only a dream. And I
am chilled speechless this morning, racked by coughing,
unable to remember. My whole body feels stiff, paralyzed
with a memory of fear, imagined touch, rough skin, a smell

on my hand. Stiff with fright, I say nothing. How do I explain a nightmare with such waking terror?

I say nothing and still she knows something has happened. At breakfast he enters the sunlit room and I collapse in a fit of coughing. He blushes, red-faced, leaves the room. There is nothing to say. I remember nothing but the dream. She knows what I remember and what I don't. We do not speak except when she turns to say, I no longer have anything to do with him. They no longer speak. The house is silent.

This is all I remember about last night.

> *Dora suffers from a sensory hallucination, from a sensa-*
> *tion of pressure on the thorax—her denial, her refusal to*
> *take into account the existence of Herr K's sexuality and*
> *her own, leaves its trace in her feeling of suffocation.*

First we remember the sounds, the smells, the single image flash arrested. Criminal injuries recorded in her. Dora coughs and coughs until her head falls off.

Dora suffers
        (Dora hallucinates?)
Dora's thorax senses
A pressure
Account
        (her denial?)
        (her sexuality?)
        (Herr K's?)

Its trace
Her suffocation
Period

Something, to be sure, has the body as its theatre.

[*from Dora's journal*] **August 13**

Since the key was stolen, I've not slept more than two or three hours at night. Most often I drift off and a small sound in the house unsettles me enough to awaken my thoughts to nothing but the terror of listening for him to come.

My asthma is getting worse and worse. There is nothing for it but to cough and cough and hope my lungs will not collapse from the weight of air bellowing inside of me.

My vagina is pouring with a white liquid, itchy and smelling like a foul dank place. I remember this from when I was smaller and Father came at night to talk with me and touch me on my breasts to see whether they were growing. Sometimes he would take off my nightgown and lie down beside me saying he was certain I was growing into a woman, but in order to ensure I would grow into a *beautiful* woman, it was necessary to make my body know the sensations of a woman's body. This was his secret; *his* father passed this down from *his* father which explained the long tradition of beautiful women in my family. He would tell me to go to sleep beside him and I would close my eyes and drift into a dream that something bad was happening but always when I woke up, Father would tell me how good I was and how he wanted me to believe in him and our secret beyond even death. I remember then, my lower parts would stink with stickiness running from my vagina. Nothing but disgust overcame me. Disgust. Sometimes I vomit thinking about my body, the dimension of his thighs, as I curl my belly away from his before dawn.

[*from Dora's journal*] **October 12**

Mama calls me a "wild creature tamed." Now that I'm sick and weak with coughing, I'm no longer "trouble." Mama tells me Father's sick now 'cause he's a lost man. She tells me he's contagious. Every day she washes out his room with disinfectant. None of us can visit him in his office. She says he's not only dying, he's death. She says she's going to die too.

I miss Father. Miss him coming to my room. Sometimes when I wake up in the middle of the night, my whole body frozen in forgetting, I want him to come to me. But now he can't and yesterday, I found my sheets bloody with cutting. The kind of stars my mother taught me how to make with the triangle crisscrossing through the centre sparkle, red across my breasts. Medals, I tell myself, medals of my own doing. My own secret battle—wounds and rewards at once.

Today my words sound as though I could die. But these words don't mean a thing. Just words. Can't feel the words. That's why I like the way my tattoos feel. My cutting moves now across my shoulders and down my left arm crisscrossing my skin with anxious love. The wounds are quick and deeper now. Sometimes I cry. Words are coming into focus. My angry words. My killing words. My losing dying words. When my fingers catch with the skin's sharp nick, I know my tears are real.

When you tell me Herr K's advances are "neither tactless nor offensive," I don't know what to say. His seductions return to me in the shape of memories of Father. Nocturnal visitations fill out a part of me that is real and not quite real to me.

I hear my writing repeat over and over this sadness. *oh god oh god oh god* addressed to no one. My haunting will not make me believe in ghosts. My words spill into single syllables and cries. Just *Oooohhh* or *Aaaahhhh* or words to this effect.

[*from Dora's journal*] **Banff, Alberta, Canada, March 26**

Fleeing Freud, I hightail it to the mountains. Nothing to write home about but this pain. At the museum, I found a remarkable series of notes penned by Mary Schaeffer about her 1908 explorations through the Rockies. As though sister to my own musings, she writes: *The wedge had been driven in; in another year the secret places would be secret no longer.* I am in the mountains to write a book. *Where am I? Where is this place? Why have I nothing to say of the mountains?* The poetics of mountains is a politics of space according to Eli, another writer staying in this marvelous hotel. His mountains are not simply high, but *elevated.* In line with this logic of altitude, I am now about to think of myself as a writer: *I am a writer.* Insecurity keeps me humble. In spite of the fact I have already written a book, I never think of myself as a writer: I am a woman, a teacher, a good friend to some, storyteller to others—but I am in the process of becoming a writer. For several weeks, this crisis of identity also keeps me from writing. What am I doing here in this beautiful cabin with a typewriter and computer, many pens and paperclips and paper and stapler and glue and scissors? Too many tools. How can I conjure words on the page all at once? My practice of writing has always been surreptitious, hidden—furtive marks on the page when I am not quite finished doing what I ought to be doing. At home, my drawers fill with scraps and fragments, overflow with different coloured inks and pages, dated now and then or not at all. Here in the mountains I have to take myself seriously. But how? My editor, a round, somewhat famous, self-important man with glasses and "good" books scattered across his room is remote and unresponsive. He doesn't take me seriously, so why should I? Am I simply paranoid, imputing bad motives and malice to his authority? Is he simply preoccupied with his work or the elk attacks in the writer's colony? Or does he intend to beat me with his indifference, the most cutting insult he can muster.

As the story unfolds, Big Daddy withholds any in-depth commentary from me for the duration of my stay in the mountains. *Is this quality writing,* he asks imperiously, *I only like quality writing.* Fortunately I find another writer, a participant in the retreat, to consult about my work. I secretly fall in love with his generous intelligence, one of the many crushes I find myself negotiating whenever someone attends to my words and listens. (*Starved for attention,* L. will say of abuse survivors, *we always crave more and more—always too much.*) I know everyone suspects my affections when I gaze at him puppylike and pathetic, but I need this male affirmation, especially when Big Daddy, jolly raconteur, refuses to respond to my work.

One morning I complain to another writer down the trail, *The pompous ass never gives me substantive comments. The most sophisticated editing he's accomplished is repositioning my semicolons. All the mother elk are out battling the tourists, perhaps one of them will flatten him.* (*Just minor physical bruises and a solid blow to his ego. Nothing serious,* I add apologetically in case he becomes an actual ample target.)

Sympathetic but unsurprised, the writer explains, *He's an autodidact, a laudable accomplishment, but you're a girl and he's jealous of your education.* Across the room a collection of antifeminist backlash published over the past month in the name of political correctness and journalistic ethics spills over the edges of the bulletin board, a black and white quilt of smug and angry fear.

What do we expect from The Globe & Mail? We conclude our discussion dissatisfied with almost everything but our newfound status as co-conspirators.

[*from Dora's journal*] **March 28** [1]

Writing aloud, she cannot even hear herself think. A good thing too, since all of her is caught up in this ink.

> *... the pulsional incidents ...*

The all of her that can't move out of the chair or imagine a world outside the room except as cinematic perspective.

> *... language lined with flesh ...*

The way a child looks like a small adult on the street just before the car brakes squeal.

> *... hear the grain of the voice ...*

An excess of adult optimism. The green of redwood and parking lot surge to the edge of her screen.

> *... a whole carnal symphony ...*

(Words crackle here before the blank face called delete.)

Dora wants to know the antithesis of nostalgia. Cynicism? Contempt for any future? *Nostalgia is a sadness without an object.... The past it seeks has never existed except as narrative.... Nostalgia wears a distinctly utopian face, a face that turns towards a future past. This point of desire which the nostalgic seeks is in fact the absence that is the very generating mechanism of desire.*

Dora remembers. She's that kind of woman: men and women fell in love with her; she with them. Later, just men, and then women only. Some remember her eyes: others saw her as innocent yet knowing, alive with laughter, and full of charm. Circles of her desire named lovers by their first initials, as though, over time, bodies become interchangeable and singular. (This state of affairs was neither good nor unwise.)

---

1 [Ed: Dora explores how to write as an obscure object of bourgeois desire: She can only write in the third person even though she knows it is the first because in owning her history, her terror becomes something to be shared beyond the *I*. *She* does not avoid implicating *me*.]

(Dora wants you to tell her more: to slide your body along a canoe glass line to sing a damp strain at the edge of your lip. Undo your nature. The fiction of this kiss.)

In a single letter of the alphabet, she could gather herself into a sunny hillside of rural memory and experience again the thick afternoon air when s/he sucked naked melon from her sweet lips.

After another half hour or so, Dora would surface and squeal, *Tell me more.*

[*from Dora's journal*] **April 7**

Sometimes Dora would begin to drink in the afternoon, bourbon on the rocks with water, then just rocks, and around midnight, straight or bottle bottoms up. Her sentences careen with the rip of mental sea change. At night in the bar, women came to talk. Dora finds herself at a table perched on some-one else's chair, hoping to feel part of the scene though she knows she can't keep up with the speed of production, the shimmer of tongue-wagged bodies.

As she listens, her throat fills up with the coming and going of story, history no more than this cough. A tear of membrane too small. One artist circulates her photographic portraits of the fecund slime along the sea wall. Mesmerized by the colour and variety of form, Dora catalogues a lexicon of words about that substance between solid and liquid:

> *slime, sludge, gummy, glutinous, mucosity, inspissate (to thicken), jelly aspic, mucilage, gelatin, isinglass, colloid, mucous, phlegm, lava, gluten, albumen, milk, cream, syrup, treacle, gum, size, glue, paste, emulsion, soup, mud, slush, slime, ooze, curdled thick, succulent, uliginous ...*

Sweat beads her brow. Her hands feel clammy in her lap.

[*from Dora's journal*] April 16

Writing will get me out of these low-down blues. The patter of fingertips while munching stuffed grape leaves and lemon, chopped. Chunks of citrus membrane exceed my despairing thoughts in sourness.

Air and her lungs tighten underwater the first day. Mother writes to ask if I am drowning. A lifeguard wants to know if I can swim. In the pool, this body's passage mesmerizes in the glass ceiling's reflection. I swim through an evening glow of canyons watching her/me from below: arms melt aspen clouds; ample belly, breasts shimmer up and down mountainous ravines. This body she knows, remote and sometimes beautiful, is hers and yet not quite ever hers. Skin gleams through roof, then fades to pale sky light just below the water's surface.

At the lecture, two women meet to compare notes. The she-i pronoun slips between them. They have altitude/attitude to keep them composed. Dora wears soft red suede boots with lizard appliqués. Beside the Bow River, the writer covets the boots out loud. Dora curves her hand round and round in the sand making overlapping circles. A tiny precise pool at the centre fills with turquoise mountain water.

Later, the writer draws this image in ink in the middle of her page, small and off centre.

A key hole or an entrance?

[*from Dora's journal*] **May 1**

A week before the publisher's deadline, the machines break down. My computer drive is corrupted and the book disappears for a few days into strange scripts of boxes. Struggling at the keyboard to try to recuperate what is lost, my body suddenly convulses with a sickness swift and furious. After an initial gasp for air, this body turns inside out with surging vomit, as though to empty out the words. Finished, I am purged and enabled. Not purified, but no longer sick with the melancholy of his memory.

My tattoos look beautiful in this light.

[*from Dora's journal*] April 23

Once upon a time, in the middle of a life, Dora pulps beans and books to make paper sheets for her new disguise. *I've destroyed my childhood books in the new machine*, she hoots. *Now I have a new story.*

Plastering all vertical surfaces with her handmade paper, she connects up words between the textured white gaps. The writing is on the wall, but the tales are hard of hearing. Surveyed from the middle of her room, flecks of verb phrases burst through in random stories. With memory's radial sense, odd tenses follow one upon any other. Among linen fibres, scraps of sentences leak telegraphic secrets.

This is home, Dora thinks to herself. *This is my safe place, but sometimes I need wings to fly.* Smoothing wet flattened surfaces with soft palms, she moulds new shoes and a speckled paper cape. Afternoons, she invites visitors to stand in her new paper shoes. Hannah advises: *Put your arm through this loop of fibre. Try on these wings and I'll make you fly.*

A slight woman accepts this invitation, sliding forearms through paper slings which extend from the wall. Dora shouts, flapping her hands with pleasure. *Feet, what do I need them for if I have wings to fly?*

IT IS TRUE. WE SHALL. WE DO.

The woman, neither bird nor angel, extends trembling arms. Her elbows bend into a sudden cry and paper wings flutter in broken folds across her breasts. Clouds of letters hesitate, then rise. She was the kind of woman who could listen to her history and still find a place for this future-past called "once upon a time …"

(So long. It's been good to know you. I don't have much space to write. Too much to say and not enough time. No time like the present to speak of this fleeting past now. Please excuse me. I'm winded not because I was running but simply because my breath is alive now.)

Fragments of an Analysis

To be peopled by one's masculine side, one's feminine side, one's inner child: it becomes conceptually crowded.... Some of us have only had dogs within. We just open our mouths and howl.

SHAWNA DEMPSEY AND LORRI MILLAN

The situation is all the more complex in that the case is offered as a 'fragment,' and this in a number of different senses: first, the case was broken off by the patient; second, it was not committed to writing until after the completion of the treatment (only the words of the dreams were recorded immediately after the session); and third, as a corollary to the second factor, only the results of the analysis and not its process were transcribed.

JACQUELINE ROSE

Women, aphasic, your life has taken place between the lines, between the sheets of paper. Torched for flaming his desire, set high on the pier to roast more slowly, sizzling and savory ...

   Eliminate the details, but the flesh remembers.

JACQUELINE DUMAS

CASE I:

The voyage within can be an exploration in abjection. In spite of the many satisfying moments of comfort and the fact that good therapy probably saved my life, sometimes I found myself sitting on a chintz couch or a leather chair or perched on a floor cushion resenting the conversation. Talk about "the child within" drove me wild with fury—as though history were a series of transparent layers to be peeled off one by one—an infinite regression into a pitiful vulnerability where the tiniest of the tiniest dolls might emerge to tell the truth, mouth painted a sweet sweet confessional smile.

The therapist dismisses my concern: *The 'child within' is only a metaphor.*

I'm supposed to ignore my knowledge about how the metaphors we live by shape how we imagine our world. The "child" in me is not a child at all, but simply someone who wasn't heard. In our culture, the figure of the child has a lot in common with the woman who speaks into the wind; in spite of experience and accomplishments, the problem of legitimacy persists. The culture's unwillingness to listen to those imagined as less worthy of a voice is not about scale and chronology but a crisis of language, power, and the body.

CASE II:

In a group exercise during a session with the therapist in residence, we are asked to draw ourselves as bounded by some imaginary border. Thinking Celtic moors, I draw a low stone wall; the solid face, overgrown with moss, is interrupted by narrow beams of light that shine through chinks in the surface. The therapist registers her concern, *Oh dear, you're not very confident of your boundaries are you?*

I sigh audibly, fed up with playing dumb, but I say nothing. Why? It doesn't make sense. She has her own utopian ideas about what makes a good boundaried image. My mortarless stone wall remains a suspicious visual metaphor. Silently I trace the pattern of fallen stones that remind me how my body can find her way to clamber over to hike through fields at will. I'm pleased that this midlife image is informed by time and decay. My world won't be bounded by the prefab equivalent of a fortress wall, or a garden gate.

CASE III:

While the therapist's work is skillful and integral to my recovery, I later become disenchanted when she announces that she doesn't disbelieve another patient who talks to "alters" who may or may not be extraterrestrial. I question her to ensure I've not misheard, but she repeats herself. Why don't I piously outline the dangers of mistaking mysticism for clarity?

In approaching the mysteries of my mind, I need a safe and steady hand to hold onto. When I take hold of a mystic's hand, my palm sweats. I tremble. (Does this therapist's hand tremble in the delicate knowledge of her power?)

My disillusionment contributes to my own healing since I can separate more easily from the vulnerable dependency I feel.

CASE IV:

The pamphlet *Self-Help Advice for the Depressed* is enough to kill me.

Depression: What You Need to Know

9. Forget about trying to read technical or complicated material—you need your concentration to do this—stick to light novels and *People* magazine.

10. Be careful about television—comedy and cartoons are okay, but anything else can depress you even more than you are.

11. If you have some work, do it in the afternoon or early evening. Your energy and interest are best at these times. Forget about the mornings.

12. Try and keep busy, but only with projects that involve your hands, not your head.

13. When you start to get better, you will notice a few minutes or more of feeling quite normal, but it doesn't last.

CASE V:

Can't stop reading about the body and memory. Want to write more ... about hysteria to blow apart the psychoanalytic mystification of desire and seduction. The equivocation in Freud's seduction theory masks fundamental refusals to validate women's stories of abuse. Memories of the crimes are so eagerly wiped out by both the perpetrator and desperate victims.

My own analysis returns: the years my beautiful analyst lounged behind me in her chair, taking notes and sighing, *whether real or imagined, the effects are the same.* The effects may be "the same" but the analysis, the cure, the recovery, the writing, the history, the facts, the touch, the legal and ethical issues, the family dynamics ... nothing is the same after the revelation.

While dismayed with the contradictions of this analytic model, the unambivalent alternative of other therapies doesn't appeal. Imagine the therapist as Girl Guide, whistle and compass shepherding her through time. The point of the exercise is singular. To feel better one identifies origin and source. The language is religious, an epiphanic journey flows from crisis to transformation to the spectre of getting stuck, crucified. But the spiralling interconnections of the past refuse the singular strobe of her flashlight that blinks on with the short-lived tenacity of a battery on high.

CASE VI:

Nineteenth-century psychoanalyst Janet hypnotized his patients to convince them the source of their trauma never occurred. X no longer suffered paralysis or hysterical fugues as a result of her father's incestuous rapes. *Your father,* Janet's hypnotic voice intoned, *did not rape you.* Patient X began to walk again, or to talk or to concentrate without the vacant stares of "spells." Freud dissimulated in other ways to stay in business. Lies made sense under the circumstances.

Freud writes about my initial telling: *This first account may be compared to an unnavigable river whose stream is at one moment choked by masses of rock and at another divided and lost among shallows and sandbanks.* His words help crystallize my own understanding of bodily symptoms: the paralysis, repetitions of language and relentless silences—the theatre of flesh and bone in which I perform.

But make no mistake: don't ask us to give up the facticity of our stories meekly. While reconstructed in the present, our reminiscences are something more than dissimulation. Our hystorical lives don't inevitably lie.

CASE VII:

What is the difference between the spectacular exhibitionism of the North-American talk shows and my desire to write about autobiographical incest narratives? How do we distinguish between Oprah and Geraldo and Sally, etc.? How many times do we rehearse our revulsion, empathy, and rage, before we find ourselves without care? What is the difference between a witness and a tourist?

> By positioning survivors who are believed, [Oprah] Winfrey makes a space for survivor discourse. This does not mean that Winfrey's position offers a "solution" to the reactionary politics of the False Memory Syndrome Foundation. Totalizing theories do not effect progressive social change. For this reason, the problem of sexual abuse and its aftereffects cannot be solved by one person, one idea, one moment, one word, one wish, one master theory, or one television production.

Popular women's magazines triumphantly publicize stories about a beautiful young woman who, inspired by a single kiss on the lips, falls for her father's sexual advances. The incestuous daughter charts their father/daughter erotic journey. The author refuses to speak about her book to the press, says her husband, an aspiring writer, who gives us his version of her words. The incestuous father, a minister, explains away his advances and argues that *God has ordained their union*. We are invited to interpret the narrative according to the cultural myth of the seductive daughter as the article continues: *She is also desperately curious to discover who her father is, and desperate that he discover her. If she becomes his victim, then she is complicit in her victimization—they both fall into the pool of obsession.*

A fashion magazine introduces a feminist historian, a fan of popular culture who likes to shop. Comparing contemporary accounts of child sexual abuse to the somatized world of Freud's nineteenth-century hysterics, she diagnoses what ails us: *A century after Freud, many people still believe psychosomatic disorders are illegitimate and search for physical evidence that firmly places cause and cure outside the self.* But her writing doesn't take into account those of us who wouldn't deny the hysterical connections our somatic symptoms speak with such unconscious authority.

CASE VIII:

Once known for its groundbreaking popularizing of women's issues, *Chatelaine* magazine publishes an article on incest as *issue of the month* in order to explore *the war raging around recovered memories.* The language of war signals what is at stake has little to do with the abused child. While the article claims to be even-handed, it accomplishes a covert goal of the False Memory Foundation—to make survivor's stories illegitimate—in this case even when they are unmediated by memory work.

In response to the article, Sylvia Fraser, author of the groundbreaking 1987 incest narrative *My Father's House* protests her misrepresentation as someone who may have misremembered her incestuous history. She writes: *my memories returned spontaneously ... at a time when any mention of incest, in or out of therapy, would have been unusual. The fact of my abuse was later independently corroborated.*

The False Memory Syndrome Foundation was founded by an alcoholic father and a mother in order to defend against their daughter's accusations. Dr. Jennifer Freyd, the abused daughter, works on "betrayal trauma theory" and writes how it developed from her personal experience and scientific expertise. When her initial accusations are dismissed, her voice is made illegitimate in spite of her international reputation. She is moved to ask:

> *Is my father more credible than me because I have a history of lying or not having a firm grasp on reality? No, I am a scientist whose empirical work has been replicated in laboratories around this country and Europe.... Am I not believed because I am a woman? A "female in her thirties" as some of the newspaper articles seem to emphasize? Am I therefore a hopeless hysteric by defini-*

> tion? Is it because the issue is father-daughter incest and,
> as my father's property, I should be silent? ... Indeed,
> why is my parents' denial at all credible? In the end, is it
> precisely because I was abused that I am to be discred-
> ited despite my personal and professional success?

Some anthropologists and feminists pursue incest's rela-
tion to the patriarchal family and the daughter as "property,"
suggesting that the incest taboo is nothing more than a way
to ensure that damaged goods are not offered to the exoga-
mous men beyond familial kin. Under heterosexual patriarchy, "the traffic in women" between men dictates: *the father
must not desire the daughter for that threatens to remove him
from the homosexual commerce in which women are exchanged
between men, in the service of power relations and community
for men.*

While this analysis flies in the face of social conservatives
who interpret the breakdown of the traditional patriarchal
family as the source of all evils, it is worth exploring why talk
of incest brings such extraordinary anxiety. Not only do public revelations about incest highlight specific incidences of
child abuse, but the controversy unmasks the structures of
authority that maintain traditional domestic relations, a dangerous threat to the status quo.

CASE IX:

The status quo has a long history. In the eighteenth– and nineteenth–centuries, obsessions about masturbation and the continual policing of children's sexuality acted not as a prohibition, but as an incitement to incest. This public and professional (medical, legal, psychological) concern with children's sexuality did not necessarily protect the child. Rather it simply provided the public with a highly charged sexualized context in which to perceive children.

Within the context of patriarchal families, incest is both *solicited and refused; it is an object of obsession and attraction, a dreadful secret and an indispensable pivot. It is manifested as a thing that is strictly forbidden in the family … ; but it is also a thing that is continuously demanded in order for the family to be a hotbed of constant sexual incitement.*

This tension between prohibition and incitement operates on the Incest.com website. Under the heading *incest,* you read the following:

> *Incest sometimes innocently results from intimate family love. Father-daughter, mother-son and brother-sister incestuous thoughts and fantasies are frequently a healthy part of growing up. The emotions and activities, love and sex in various guises, can seem ok and even good at the time. The problems revolve around the change in relationship that incest actions bring. We want to speak freely and openly about intense family love. We openly deal with an aspect of human relationships that long has been treated as unspeakable.*

Meanwhile a hyperlink to an advertisement for the Incest.com site reads:

We NOW offer the most inflammatory material available anywhere. The materials are so explicit and graphic that ads for them were banned from New York City's notorious cable channel J.

CASE X:

What triggers disaster? How do we distinguish between malice and the inertia of this historical moment? Jacqueline Rose's comments help me understand:

> In order to insist on the reality of child sexual abuse (something which can still be fervently and religiously denied), you pay a conceptual price. In one, dominant set of representations, a symbolic shift—partly a reflexing of old images—has taken place. The child victim is desexualized—necessarily—for there does not seem to be a readily available language in which one can talk of childhood sexuality and insist on the reality of child sexual abuse at the same time. Language itself is made innocent—since children can only be made to talk of abuse with great difficulty, it is essential to believe them when they do (in cases of alleged child sexual abuse, the idea that there might be play, fantasy or ambiguity in language is almost invariably used to discredit the child). It is essential, too, that the child's voice be clear and unequivocal in order to lift the adult burden of disbelief. More important still, if damage to children can be shown to stem from lone abusers, then the wider culture—with its responsibilities, trials and dangers in relation to children—can be absolved. Thus childhood returns to pre-Freudian state of sexual innocence and families, that is, families without abusers, revert to the ideal.

CASE XI:

In a culture fascinated with and fearful of sexuality, it makes sense that one of the driving forces of social order would be the insistence on heterosexuality as a "natural" good. Tonight even melodrama can't dampen my rage, head peppered with appalling stories of right-wing legislators who wring life out of the poor, the curious, the artistic—while grandstanding on behalf of their own brute ignorance.

As I edit this manuscript, Alberta life is dominated by conversations about the Supreme Court of Canada ruling to protect the human rights of homosexuals. Provincial politicians plot about how to maintain "the family" untainted by nontraditional forms. A foster mother who has nourished over 70 children is prohibited from fostering because in the middle of her life she has fallen in love with a woman—as though mothering were a question of sexual desire. In response to this state-enforced bigotry, a lesbian friend chooses exile over childlessness and decides to leave the province in order to adopt. If the wellbeing of children were uppermost in the government's thoughts, they might be concerned that since welfare cuts in 1993, the number of children in foster care increased almost 50 percent. Newspaper headlines read: *Poverty blamed for rise in kids taken into care: Alberta growth rate leads the nation*, and yet the Social Services minister denies the impact of poverty on children and diverts our attention to more pressing moral conundrums like sexual orientation.

The insistence on maintaining a narrow definition of the family reinforces the erroneous association of homosexuality with pedophilia. The villains are *perverts* or *lone abusers* outside the traditional family circle. However the easy opposition of this moral tale falters when we examine those who abuse— more often than not upstanding god-fearing heterosexuals.

CASE XII:

> *The very act of speaking out has become used as performance and spectacle. The growth of this phenomenon raises questions: has it simply replayed confessional modes which recuperate dominant patriarchal discourses without subversive effect, or has it been able to create new spaces within these discourses and to begin to develop an autonomous counterdiscourse, one capable of empowering survivors?*

Somewhere between hysteria and hoax, this manuscript bounces from pillar to post, dances from editor to editor, awaiting a listening ear. Prose publishers tell me it is too experimental—*Why not try a poetry publisher?* Poetry publishers tell me the manuscript is especially fine, just not poetry. Others explain how the incest narrative has had its day—now they crave something more lucrative, upbeat and inspiring. *When are there too many war stories?* a friend inquires.

On the telephone, another writer conveys her discouragement: *Everyone wants a happy pill. But little has changed. Have we stopped the abuse from continuing? Have we done anything more than heal a few individual women, sometimes unwittingly collaborating with a conservative pro-family agenda. Where are the convictions? The effective education? The treatment and support?*

Meanwhile, I interview women who have written about child sexual abuse. My shock at the number of fictive stories that turn out to be rooted in fact becomes compassion when months later several women call to tell me they want to rebury their revelations—for the sake of their daughter or son, their mother or grandfather, their father or uncle. The urge to conceal secrets maintains peace within the family.

CASE XIII:

In the room, seven women tell their stories. The details are not repeatable, but imagine the way the skin crawls and creeps with fear, the crinkle of sheets or blankets as unwanted hands move beneath. The unwanted glimpses of his body; his look, a blow. Her uncaring indifference or just plain silence. The knowledge of surveillance. Her refusal to speak on behalf of ... in defence of ... against. The house is small, in the country, in the city, or large in the suburbs. The child is young. Too young to remember? Or the child is big enough to look like a woman. The child is a woman about to become a child again and speak.

As they speak their story, the women say over and over how they want to find a way to make the wounds bind and heal over. Our healing is homeopathic: we "identify" and recognize ourselves in the other's suffering.

During the session, the woman across the room scares me so I say, *If you write, perhaps you will find a way to stop yourself from self-mutilation.*

While others are at lunch, I apologize to the therapist for interpreting another woman's pain. *Are you suicidal,* she asks and I look at her more closely now.

It's hard to say the words when your father has drowned himself. I have the desire ... yes, I suppose....

I like to look directly into suicide, she says. *What do you want to kill.*

Taken aback, I think *if I risk the EXIT door, who else will know?*

At the end of the afternoon, we are all asked to enact our trauma in front of the others—to make amateur drama out of the dread we have hidden within. But to perform our stories is to reengage with the pain and we refuse to do as we are told. *All of us have had enough suffering for the day*, says one woman. *If we want catharsis, it's cheaper for us to go the theatre.* The rest of us nod our heads in silent agreement

Why reenact the trauma when our fear is so accessible to us? MB observes wryly: *I don't know of any revolution started by this kind of therapy. You're never going to heal by picking at your scabs.* Later that night, I creep to bed to relive the fear, their fear, to enact my own fear of betrayal, inevitable loss of love, and uncomprehending abandonment.

We gather to listen to the stories. Details are confidential. True to each other, in confidence, we speak. Now all that matters is that this writing refuses to document, record and reveal their words. All that matters is vagueness, abstraction, and indeterminate scenes. All that matters is that I refuse to locate myself anywhere but in this I. A small story through which I exit from an old empire of fear.

Where Does the Misery Come From?

It is a matter of changing the horizon itself.

The first night she returned to her father's cottage to edit the galleys of her book, she scanned the autograph wall to find her own melodramatic pencilled scrawl that read "Pelican Lake, you sang to me in my aloneness. August 13 1969." Now almost thirty years later, as her canoe approached the point, the lake's current pulled her towards the open water beyond. She felt her father's presence as she walked the length of the windswept beach scanning shale fragments for signs of buffalo teeth and flint arrow heads. The timbre of his voice caught her by surprise, echoing a less remote forgotten history. In her journal she wrote:

> *She was certain it was true and then had her doubts. These doubts were impossible to locate except as denial, fear, repudiation. Or insight? These doubts embarrassed, no, alarmed. The uncertainty principle does not apply. Do not apply uncertainty to these thoughts for fear they will come back to haunt you as guilt. Guilt does not apply. I am not guilty or fearful or bad. I am uncertain about the past and filled with eager anticipation of a future to be determined.*

All week long she avoided the manuscript and haunted local junk stores to remake the cottage in her own image: a green jaguar lamp restored for protection; foggy wall mirror mounted to hold water and light; fuzzy chenille bedspread and lace curtains to tame her dreams; green and red Hudson's Bay blankets for the child's bed; a toy box rehinged to store new blocks and boats for play. At week's end, she arranged the yard-sale chair and grey metal typewriter table with a view of the water to illuminate her new writing.

On the far bedroom wall her father's old jackets hung on twisted-wire hooks. His scent no longer filled the sleeves, but she couldn't bear their sight all night long, so she folded them into the bottom drawer of the pale carved bureau she found in the Brandon pawn shop. Savouring the scent of lemon and water, she had scrubbed out the drawers to wash away fingerprints of another domestic life.

Last month, when she received notice that her formal application had reached Bejiing, she burst inexplicably into tears. *Oh you're having an hysterical pregnancy*, a friend joked affectionately. It was true: her womb was about to wander all the way to China. In January, she would travel with her mother to bring her daughter home. Enthusiastically, but without much success, she was learning Cantonese—the word for mother that sounded like "maw" mixed itself up with a low tonal variation indicating a question. Already, her nieces squealed in delightful anticipation as they called her "Rae" after their grandmother, and their mother and maternal aunt. But all of them knew "Rae" would already have a name she would continue to claim as her own.

On the upper shelf of the boathouse, brightly coloured water wings and life jackets await their return next summer when she will teach her daughter to swim.

The only way we can find our way is through the bush. Dense. Impossible.
Until the moment we reach the meadow when we have arrived.
Until the moment the meadow, crossed is now remembered as we enter the bush again.

Acknowledgments

This book is dedicated to my mother Olive, to my brothers Ward and Scott, and to the future of my well-loved nieces and nephews Elliot Rachel and Noah Alexander Williamson, Lucy MacKenzie, and the Balmy Beach clan. I write thinking with love of a sparkle in the western sky.

This writing journey has been helped by many. Daring women and men who confronted their painful histories provided me with a path. The Banff Centre Visual Arts Residency Program and especially the generosity and wit of Jeanne Randolph and Daina Augaitis along with the computer expertise of Doug Walker made my first visual imaginings of this book possible. A Canada Council Non-Fiction Writing Grant afforded me precious uninterrupted time to tend this manuscript. The University of Alberta Department of English provided resources for some of this research. My thanks to Astrid Blodgett, Carol Kleckner, Judy Dunlop and Lisa Ward for their work. A sabbatical scholarship at the University of British Columbia Centre for Research in Women's Studies and Gender Relations offered convivial inspiration. The Alberta/Leeds Exchange and the School of English, Leeds University, especially Lynette Hunter gave me a stimulating place to write. A Social Science and Humanities Research Council Strategic Grant has enabled Lynne Bell and me to investigate prairie women's cultural work and social change, a project that has inspired this writing.

My thanks to Lynne Bell for her walks, talks, mutually wild laughter, and collaborative intelligence. This book would not have been accomplished over the past seven years without the following generous friends and manuscript readers: Mary Chapman, Kim Echlin, Debbie Gorham, Garry Spotowski, Lola Lemire Tostevin, Isabel Huggan,

Angela Julian, Jane Arscott, Lise Gotell, Cathy Bray, Elizabeth MacKenzie, Mark Czarnecki, Gary Watson, Pauline Butling, Fred Wah, Claudine Potvin, Elly Danica, Daphne Marlatt, Di Brandt, Chris Wiesenthal, Susan Shirriff, Cathy Chilco, Jeff Taylor, Colette Urban, Jocelyn Robert, Stan Dragland and Don McKay. The good cheer of Kyoko Sato, Andrea Katz, Ellen Quigley, Rob Gray, Shazia Rahman, Mari Sasano and Guy Beauregard provided me with healing laughter during my illness. Diana Hartog's slip of the tongue named this book "crybaby." Special thanks to Heather Bain, Orval Henderson, Cheryl Malmo, Carol Gannom, Vivien Smith and the gathering of women with whom I shared my stories. Miss Phoebe and the late Monsieur Mars (Chien) performed splendid "inner dogs."

Parts of this manuscript in various forms have been presented at Sookmyung Women's University, University of Seoul, University of Taejon, Korean Women's Literature Association (Seoul), Universidad de la Laguna (Tenerife, Islas Canarias), The Institute of Common-wealth and American Studies and English Language (Mysore), University of Bombay, S.N.D.T. Women's University University (Bombay), University of Delhi, Orlando Books (Edmonton), University of Alberta, University of Calgary, Annual Conference of the Association for Canadian Studies in German-Speaking Countries (Grainau, Germany), University of Goa (Panajii), University of British Columbia, Canadian Women's Studies Association, "Re: Verse/Re: Vision: A Canadian Feminist Poetry Conference" (Winnipeg) and The Body Conference at the University of Saskatchewan. My thanks to the organizers of these occasions.

I am grateful to the writer-friendly NeWest Press and to the follow-ing who published earlier versions of this writing: Nicole Markotic and Ashok Mathur, editors of *Altitude x 2,* disOrientation Press; David Arnason, Turnstone Press; Wendy Waring and the Women's Press Editors of *By, For and About: Feminist Cultural Politics;* Wendy Pullen and the editorial collective of *A Room of One's Oswn;* and Ivan Sundal, editor of *Our Fathers: Poetry and prose by daughters and sons from the prairies* where a series of the computer-generated photos first appeared.

Works Cited

The only book that is ... Hélène Cixous. *Three Steps on the Ladder of Writing.* Trans. Sarah Cornell and Susan Sellers. New York: Columbia U, 1993.

Shadow seemed to lie across the page ... Virginia Woolf. *A Room of One's Own.* London: Granada, 1977.

Writing isn't just telling stories ... Marguerite Duras. *Practicalities.* Trans. Barbara Bray. New York: Grove Weidenfeld, 1990.

CRYBABY!

Like this exclamation mark ... bpNichol. "slip." *Gifts: The Martyrology Book[s] 7 & 8.* Toronto: Coach House Press, 1990.

Cry, crybaby ... *The Compact Edition of the Oxford English Dictionary.* London: Oxford, 1971. Unless otherwise noted, all other definitions and etymologies are from this edition.

The language of pain ... Diane Wakoski. "Civilization." *Talking Poetry: Conversations in the Workshop with Contemporary Poets.* Ed. Lee Bartlett. Albuquerque: U of New Mexico, 1987.

What is the reason that as soon as ... Simone Weil. *Gravity and Grace.* London: Routlege, 1992.

SNAPSHOTS

The camera saves a set ... John Berger. *Another Way of Telling.* New York: Pantheon, 1982.

Somewhere someone has taken my identity ... Theresa Hak Kyung Cha. *Dictee.* New York: Tanam P, 1982.

The family photograph is a ritual of the domestic cult ... Pierre Bourdieu. *Photography: A Middle-brow Art.* Trans. Shaun Whiteside. California: Stanford UP, 1990.

In a half dream state ... Months later, the second telling ... In the cedar V of the mountains ... Revised from Janice Williamson. *Tell Tale Signs.* Winnipeg: Turnstone P, 1991.

Always watch your backgrounds ... Thomas H. Miller and Wyatt Brummitt. *This is Photography: Its Means and Ends.* Garden City, New York: Garden City Books, 1955.

Father provided his own kind of shopping pleasures ... Janice Williamson. "Notes from Storyville North." *Life Style Shopping: The Subject of Consumption.* Ed. Rob Shields. New York: Routledge, 1991.

Story-telling sequence pictures ... Nowadays, the aim of a family photo ... Better Homes and Gardens Photography for your family. Des Moines: Meredith P, 1964.

In place of bigness, ... Thomas H. Miller and Wyatt Brummitt. *This is Photography: Its Means and Ends.*

Children: Being like young animals, ... Eric de Maré. *Photography.* Baltimore: Penguin, 1971.

In its presentation of identity ... Daphne Marlatt. "On Distance and Identity: Ten Years Later." *Steveston.* Edmonton: Longspoon, 1984.

You can show yourself in a reckless role ... Better Homes and Gardens: Photography for your family.

The trick is to align both figures ... Better Homes and Gardens Photography for your family.

The impact of incest may be hidden ... In Dora's Case: Freud–Hysteria–Feminism. Eds. Charles Bernheimer and Claire Kahane. New York: Columbia UP, 1985.

The I am is given its time in which to reflect ... John Berger "Paul Strand." *About Looking.* New York: Vintage, 1991.

First she takes off ... Janice Williamson. *Altitude x 2.* Calgary: DisOrientation, 1992.

Habit now protects us ... John Berger. "Uses of Photography." *About Looking.*

It is beyond the shock of being stricken, ... Shoshana Felman. "Education and Crisis, or the Vicissitudes of Teaching."

Testimony: Crises of Witnessing. New York: Routledge, 1992.

To testify is to encounter ...   Shoshana Felman. *Testimony.*

Children who have been abused ...   Susan Griffin. from "The First and the Last: A Woman Thinks About War." *The American Voice* 13.

TATTOO

A photograph can certainly throw you off the scent ...   Annette Kuhn. "Reminiscences." *Family Snaps: The Meanings of Domestic Photography.* Eds. Jo Spence and Patricia Holland. London: Virago, 1991.

Art, like dermatology, is fundamentally about ...   Barbara Marie Stafford. *Body Criticism: Imaging the Unseen in Enlightenment Art and Medicine.* Cambridge, Mass: MIT Press, 1991.

Tattoo ...   *The New Lexicon Webster's Encyclopedic Dictionary of the English Language.* New York: Lexicon Publications, 1988.

The blood looked very satisfactory ...   Marian Engel. "The Tattooed Woman," *The Tattooed Woman.* Markham: Penguin, 1985.

Welts, scars, cuts, ...   Elizabeth Grosz. *Volatile Bodies: Toward a Corporeal Feminism.* Indiana UP, 1994.

SWING MEMORY

To articulate the past historically ...   Walter Benjamin. "Theses on the Philosophy of History." *Illuminations.* Trans. Larry Zohn. New York: Schocken Books, 1969.

There is a pain —so utter— ...   Emily Dickinson. No. 599. *The Complete Poems of Emily Dickinson.* Ed. Thomas H. Johnson. Toronto: Little Brown, 1960.

Trauma is always the story of a wound ...   Cathy Caruth. *Unclaimed Experience: Trauma, Narrative, and History.* Baltimore: John Hopkins UP, 1996.

A crisis of reminiscences ...   Freud writes that "Hysterics suffer mainly from reminiscences." qtd. *In Dora's Case.*

I am fanned by the wings of memory.   From an art installation by Joane Cardinal Schubert. *Indigenia.* National Gallery of Canada. Edmonton Art Gallery, 1992.

An unused memory gets lost, ceases to exist,... Christa Wolf.
   Patterns of Childhood. Trans. Ursule Molinaro and Hedwig
   Rappolt. New York: Farrar, Straus and Giroux, 1980.

Here and here alone ... Monique David-Ménard. *Hysteria from
   Freud to Lacan: Body and language in psychoanalysis.* Trans.
   Catherine Porter. Ithaca: Cornell UP, 1989.

A woman's memory then ... Gail Scott. *Spaces Like Stairs.* Toronto:
   Women's Press, 1989.

There is something about the body of the other ... *In Dora's Case.*

He goes on to look for yet another ... Monique David-Ménard.
   Hysteria from Freud to Lacan.

The displacement of sensations ... *In Dora's Case.*

"**Listen.**" Daphne Marlatt. *Networks: Selected Poems.* Ed. Fred Wah.
   Vanouver: Talonbooks, 1980.

Halfway ... Sigmund Freud. "Studies on Hysteria." *The Standard
   Edition.* Trans. J. Strachey. London: Hogarth P, 1955.

Before they come for analysis,... Freud. qtd. Elaine Showalter.
   Hystories: Hysterical Epidemics and Modern Media. New York:
   Columbia, 1997.

In the mind one forms ... Mary Carruthers. *The Book of Memory:
   A Study of Memory in Medieval Culture.* Cambridge: Cambridge
   UP, 1990.

There are many things we know ... Susan Griffin. from "The First
   and the Last: A Woman Thinks About War."

We are unable to remember traumatic events ... Joseph E. LeDoux.
   "Emotion, Memory and the Brain." *Scientific American* (June 1994).

There may also be a thoroughly ... Ian Hacking. *Rewriting the Soul:
   Multiple Personality and the Sciences of Memory.* Princeton:
   Princeton UP, 1995.

The historical truth of a woman writer's life ... Nancy Miller.
   "Women's Autobiography in France: For a Dialectics of
   Identification." *Women and Language in Literature and Society.* Eds.
   Sally McConnell-Ginet *et al.* New York: Praeger Publishers, 1980.

Fiction is a transgression ... *Guardian Weekly* (April 3, 1994) 150.14.

You must forget it all ... Guardian Weekly.

Nobody ever told me the war was over.... Binjamin Wilkomirski.
Fragments: Memories of a Wartime Childhood. Trans. Carol Brown
Janeway. New York: Schocken, 1996.

An Ontario survey ... Ann Duffy. "The Feminist Challenge:
Knowing and Ending the Violence." *Feminist Issues: Race, Class
and Sexuality.* Ed. Nancy Mandell. 2nd ed. Scarborough: Prentice
Hall, 1998.

The scene is not merely ... Ian Hacking. *Rewriting the Soul.*

Innocence is not a property of childhood ... Jacqueline Rose. *The
Case of Peter Pan or The Impossibility of Children's Fiction.*
Philadelphia: U of Pennsylvania P, 1984.

Work and its "work" ... Elaine Scarry. *The Body in Pain: The
Making and Unmaking of the World.* Toronto: Oxford UP, 1985.

PUMPS

Melancholy persons are foreigners ... Julia Kristeva. *Black Sun:
Depression and Melancholia.* Trans. Leon S. Roudiez. New York:
Columbia UP, 1989.

Mother's shoes her pumps ... Janice Williamson. *Tell Tale Signs.*

It's day, everything is about to begin ... Marguerite Duras. *The
Malady of Death: Five Novels.* New York: Grove P, 1985.

If I did not agree to lose mother, ... Julia Kristeva. *Black Sun:
Depression and Melancholia.*

THE FATHER ROOM

That is a Dead Father, ... Donald Barthelme. *The Dead Father.*
New York: Farrar, Strans and Girous, 1975.

You do not distinguish the boulder that buries you ... Christa Wolf.
Patterns of Childhood. Trans. Ursule Molinaro and Hedwig
Rappolt. New York: Farrar, Straus and Giroux, 1980.

The disaster is related to forgetfulness ... Maurice Blanchot. *The Writing of Disaster.* Trans. Ann Smock. Lincoln: U of Nebraska P, 1986.

Monster as etymologically ambiguous is discussed in Louis Marin.

Utopics: The Semiological Play of Textual Spaces. Trans. Roberta A. Vollrath. Atlantic Highlands, NJ: 1984.

And now it's the mouth ... Kim Morrisey. *Poems for Men Who Dream of Lolita.* Saskatoon: Coteau Books, 1992.

The anxiety provoked ... A definition of the 'uncanny' in Shoshana Felman. *What Does a Woman Want? Reading and Sexual Difference.* Baltimore: John Hopkins, 1993.

Hush, don't speak, the sea doesn't like it ... Marie Cardinal. *The Words to Say It.* Trans. Pat Goodheart. Cambridge: Van Vactor & Goodheart, 1983.

For those whose fathers considered suicide only to drown ... Janice Williamson. *Tell Tale Signs.*

The sea has a tendency to beguile ... Hirokazu Kore-eda. Maborosi (Maborosi ino Hikart, 1995).

Who is this patient ... Ian Hacking. *Rewriting the Soul.*

The border is a swing door ... France Theoret. *The Tangible Word.* Trans. Barbara Godard. Montreal: Guerenica, 1991.

To read without writing ... St. Jerome qtd. in Mary Carruthers. *The Book of Mermory: A Study of Memory in Medieval Culture.*

But my father, my beloved and most wretched father? ... Mary Wollstonecraft Shelley. "Mathilda." *The Mary Shelley Reader.* Eds. Betty T. Bennett and Charles E. Robinson. New York: Oxford UP, 1990.

She transmits a tale ... Tilottama Rajan. "Mary Shelley's Mathilda: Melancholy and the Political Economy of Romanticism." *Studies in the Novel* 26.2 (1994).

Disgusting and detestable, ... William Godwin qtd. in Karen Jacobsen McLennan. "Introduction." *Nature's Ban: Women's Incest Literature.* Boston: Northeastern UP: 1996.

EKTOMY

Whenever we turn ... Ingeborg Bachmann. "In the Storm of Roses." *Against Forgetting: Twentieth-Century Poetry of Witness.* Ed. Carolyn Forché. New York: Norton, 1993.

I will make what does not exist,... Mary Melfi. *Infertility Rites: A Novel.* Montreal: Guernica, 1991.

She does not want to expropriate her body's suffering ... This paragraph is rooted in Hélène Cixous' writing: "Fever, which is unbearable, is a defensive phenomenon. It is a combat. It is the same thing for suffering: in suffering there is a whole manoeuvre of the unconscious, of the soul, of the body, that makes us come to bear the unbearable." Hélène Cixous and Miraille Calle-Gubar. *Rootprints: Memory and Life Writing.* Trans. Eric Prenowitz. New York: Routledge, 1997.

Mère, pleurer ... Mallarme's poetry and testimony are investigated by Felman in *Testimony.*

Trauma may lead, therefore, to the encounter with another, ... Cathy Caruth. *Unclaimed Experience: Trauma, Narrative, and History.*

Stones are old money ... Gwendolyn MacEwen qtd. in Rosemary Sullivan. *Shadow Maker: The Life of Gwendolyn MacEwen.* Toronto: Harper Collins, 1995.

The image "five stones spread on this summit" is inspired by a series of photographic performance works by Marlene Creates.

ADORABLE DORA

Dora had for some time ... Toril Moi. "Representation of Patriarchy: Sexuality and Epistemology in Freud's Dora." *In Dora's Case.* Eds. Charles Bernheimer and Claire Kahane.

I am what Dora would have been ... Hélène Cixous and Catherine Clément. *The Newly Born Woman.* Trans. Betsy Wing. Minneapolis: U of Minnesota, 1986.

The problem of the referent ... Sharon Willis. "Hélène Cixous' Portrait of Dora: The Unseen and the Un-scene." *Performing Feminisms: Feminist Critical Theory and Theatre.* Ed. Sue-Ellen Case. Baltimore: Johns Hopkins UP, 1990.

Dora suffers from a sensory hallucination,... In *Dora's Case.*

Something, to be sure,... In *Dora's Case.*

The wedge had been driven in; ... Mary Schaeffer. *A Hunter of Peace.* Ed. E.J Hart. Banff: The Whyte Foundation, 1980.

Where am I? Where is this place ... Eli Mandel. *Life Sentence: Poems and Journals: 1976–1980.* Victoria: Press Porcépic, 1981.

The pulsional incidents ... Roland Barthes. *The Pleasure of the Text.* Trans. Richard Miller, New York: Noonday P, 1980.

Nostalgia is a sadness ... Roland Barthes. *Camera Lucida: Reflections on Photography.* Trans. Richard Howard. New York: Hill and Wang, 1981.

Feet what do I need them for ... Frida Kahlo's 1953 journal entry on having her right leg amputated. *The Diary of Frida Kahlo: An Intimate Self Portrait.* Ed. Sarah M. Lowe. New York: Harry N. Abrams, 1995.

It is true. We shall. We do ... Dorothy Livesay qtd. in Rosemary Sullivan. *Shadow Maker: The Life of Gwendolyn MacEwen.*

FRAGMENTS OF ANALYSIS

To be peopled by one's ... Shawna Dempsey and Lorri Millan. "The Thin Skin of Normal." Performed as part of *Under the Skirt: a mixed media cabaret.* Edmonton: Catalyst Theatre, February 7, 1998.

The situation is all the more complex ... Jacqueline Rose. "Dora-Fragment of an Analysis." *Sexuality in the Field of Vision.* London: Verso, 1986.

Women, aphasic, your life has taken place ... Jacqueline Dumas. *Madelaine and the Angel.* Saskatoon: Fifth House, 1989.

Depression: What You Need to Know 9–13. Prepared for The Mood Disorder Service, University of British Columbia, Revised, 1991.

Your father ... did not rape you ... qtd. in Judith Lee Herman. *Trauma and Recovery.* New York: Basic Books, 1992.

This first account may be compared to an unnavigable river ... Sigmund Freud. *Dora: An Analysis of a Case of Hysteria.* Ed. Philip Reiff. New York: Macmillan, 1979.

By positioning survivors who are believed, ... Rosario Champagne.

"Oprah Winfrey's *Scared Silent* and the Spectatorship of Incest." *Discourse* 17.2 (1994–95).

God has ordained their union … She is also desperately curious to discover … Colin Harrison. "Sins of the Father." *Vogue* (April 1997).

A century after Freud, many people still … Laurie Abraham. "Diagnosis: Hysteria." *Mirabella* (March/April 1997).

The war raging around recovered memories … Sandra Martin. "You *must* remember this." *Chatelaine* 70.9 (1997).

My memories returned … "Sylvia Fraser replies." *Chatelaine* 70.11 (1997).

Is my father more credible than me … Jennifer Freyd qtd. in Rosario Champagne. "Oprah Winfrey's *Scared Silent* and the Spectatorship of Incest." See also Jennifer Freyd. *Betrayal Trauma: The Logic of Forgetting Childhood Abuse.* Cambridge: Harvard UP, 1996. For a useful survey of the clinical literature see: Susan L. Reviere. *Memory of Childhood Trauma: A Clinician's Guide to the Literature.* New York: Guildford, 1996.

The father must not desire the daughter … Jane Gallop. *The Daughter's Seduction: Feminism and Psychoanalysis.* Ithaca: Cornell UP, 1982.

Solicited and refused; it is an object of obsession and attraction, … Foucault quoted in Vikki Bell. *Interrogating Incest: Feminism Foucault and the Law.* New York: Routledge, 1993.

Incest sometimes innocently … Incest.com. April 1998.

We NOW offer … Incest.com. April 1998.

In order to insist on the reality of child sexual abuse … Jacqueline Rose. *The Case of Peter Pan.*

Poverty blamed … Mike Sadava. "Poverty blamed for rise in kids taken into care." *The Edmonton Journal* (April 14, 1998). Alberta is the only province in Canada that refused to approve the United Nations Convention on the Rights of the Child.

The very act of speaking out has become used as performance … Linda Alcoff and Laura Gray. "Survivor Discourse: Transgression or Recuperation" *Signs* 18.2 (1993).

I don't know of any revolution … Marjorie Beaucage in Lynne Bell and Janice Williamson. "On Crossing Lines and Going Between: An Interview with Marjorie Beaucage." *Tessera* 22 (1997).

WHERE DOES THE MISERY COME FROM?

Where does the misery come from?... Jacqueline Rose. "Psychoanalysis, Feminism, and the Event" in Pt. 11 The Death Drive of *Why War?: Psychoanalysis, Politics and the Return to Melanie Klein*. Cambridge: Blackwell, 1993.

It is a matter of changing ... Luce Irigaray. "Love Between Us." *An Ethics of Sexual Difference*. Trans. Carolyn Burke and Gillian C. Gill. Ithaca: Cornell UP, 1993.

The only way we can find ... Sharon Zukin. *Landscapes of Power: From Detroit to Disney World*. Berkeley: U of California P, 1991.